PRAISE FOR MIKE SAGER

"Sager plays Virgil in the modern American Inferno... Compelling and stylish magazine journalism, rich in novelistic detail."
—*Kirkus Reviews*

"Like his journalistic precursors Tom Wolfe and Hunter S. Thompson, Sager writes frenetic, off-kilter pop-sociological profiles of Americans in all their vulgarity and vitality . . . He writes with flair, but only in the service of an omnivorous curiosity and defies expectations in pieces that lesser writers would play for satire or sensationalism . . . A Whitmanesque ode to teeming humanity's mystical unity."
—*The New York Times Book Review*

"I once described Mike Sager as "the Beat poet of American journalism." The title is still apt. For decades, he has explored the beautiful and horrifying underbelly of American society with poignantly explicit portrayals of porn stars, swingers, druggies, movie stars, rockers and rappers, as well as stunning stories about obscure people whose lives were resonant with deep meaning—a 92-year-old man, an extraordinarily beautiful woman, a 650-pound man. He became a journalistic ethnographer of American life and his generation's heir to the work of Gay Talese, Tom Wolfe, and Hunter S. Thompson. His imposing body of work today is collected in more than a dozen books and eBooks."
—Walt Harrington, author and past head of Journalism at the University of Illinois.

"The sentences flow with a definite rhythm, but Sager's style is unadorned with falsity, unburdened by over-interpretation. He's a natural storyteller. You never get the feeling he's there just to show off, only to entertain you."
—Alex Belth, editor of EsquireClassic.com and The Stacks Reader Series

Like a silver-tongued Margaret Mead, Sager slips into foreign societies almost unnoticed and lives among the natives, chronicling his observations in riveting long-form narratives."
—*Performances Magazine*

"Sager has made a career of finding the unexpected story and telling it with empathy and narrative skill."
—*Publishers Weekly*

"His self-effacing style evokes George Orwell's famous dictum that good writing should be as transparent as a pane of glass... Exhibit A for why, in an age of video, writing still matters."
—*San Diego CityBeat*

ALSO BY MIKE SAGER

NONFICTION

Scary Monsters and Super Freaks:
Stories of Sex, Drugs, Rock 'n' Roll, and Murder

Revenge of the Donut Boys:
True Stories of Lust, Fame, Survival, and Multiple Personality

The Someone You're Not:
True Stories of Sports, Celebrity, Politics & Pornography

Stoned Again: The High Times and Strange Life of a Drugs Correspondent

Vetville: True Stories of the U.S. Marines at War and at Home

The Devil and John Holmes - 25th Anniversary Author's Edition:
And Other True Stories of Drugs, Porn and Murder

Janet's World:
The Inside Story of Washington Post Pulitzer Fabulist Janet Cooke

Travels with Bassem:
A Palestinian and a Jew Find Friendship in a War-Torn Land

The Lonely Hedonist:
True Stories of Sex, Drugs, Dinosaurs and Peter Dinklage

Tattoos & Tequila:
To Hell and Back with One of Rock's Most Notorious Frontmen

Shaman: The Mysterious Life and Impeccable Death of Carlos Castaneda

Hunting Marlon Brando: A True Story

A Boy and His Dog in Hell: And Other True Stories

The Rise and Fall of a Super Freak:
And Other True Stories of Black Men Who Made History

FICTION

Deviant Behavior, A Novel

High Tolerance, A Novel

The Pope of Pot:
And Other True Stories of Marijuana and Related High Jinks

Copyright © 2022 Mike Sager

All rights reserved. No part of this publication may be reproduced, stored in a retrieval system, or transmitted, in any form or by any means, electronic, mechanical, photocopying, recording, or otherwise, without the prior written permission of the publisher.
Published in the United States of America.

Cover design and cover art by WBYK.com.au
Interior design by Siori Kitajima, PatternBased.com

Cataloging-in-Publication data for this book
is available from the Library of Congress.
ISBN-13:
Paperback: 978-1-950154-79-1
eBook: 978-1-950154-78-4

Published by The Sager Group LLC
TheSagerGroup.net
In conjunction with NeoText
NeoTextCorp.com

THE POPE OF POT

AND OTHER TRUE STORIES OF MARIJUANA AND RELATED HIGH JINKS

MIKE SAGER

CONTENTS

Introduction: When Should a Man Stop Smoking Weed?..........1
In the course of my travels—as both a person and a journalist—marijuana has served as a great equalizer, a frequent teacher, and a pleasant companion, leading me places I would never have otherwise gone. When should a man stop smoking weed? Maybe never.

The High Life and Strange Times of the Pope of Pot................13
A pioneer of pot delivery services, Mickey the Pope had an 800 number and a corps of bicycle messengers, all of them covered by a company dental plan. Meet the marijuana pope and his faithful followers at the Church of Realized Fantasies. Too bad the cops didn't think he was so amusing.

Dab Artists..31
In the early years of legal marijuana, the craftsmen on the outlaw edge of the vaping boom worked in the shadows. They called themselves "Wooks." They extracted only the finest erl, crumble, and shatter, strictly gourmet. Cool but nerdy, deliberately unkempt, more comfortable alone or in small groups, these self-taught Heisenbergs of hash oil convened once a year for the Secret Cup Finals in Las Vegas. A look at the last days before the machinery of legalization took hold.

The Pot Doctor Will See You Now 49
At ten in the morning an alarm is chime chime chiming from a laptop in a soundproof cubicle in a Downtown LA loft space. The queue of patients is already full, a virtual line running out the door—a mom with panic disorder; a grandfather with back pain; college kid who has trouble sleeping. A long and jangled day with Dr. D., MD—the hardest working doctor in the cannabis biz.

Meeting the Ghost of Christmas Future..**55**
After a questionable police raid on his house in Woody Creek, Colorado, the legendary journalist and Rolling Stone National Affairs Chief Hunter S. Thompson is charged with possession of illegal drugs and faces a fifty-year prison sentence. A young Mike Sager is dispatched to the scene. The next three weeks will teach at least one of them lessons to last a lifetime.
    The Trial of Hunter S. Thompson..**55**
    Charges Dropped Against Hunter Thompson...................... **64**
    The Morning Coke: On Being Hunter S. Thompson's Assistant for Three Weeks... **68**

WHEN SHOULD A MAN STOP SMOKING WEED?

In the course of my travels—as both a person and a journalist—marijuana has served as a great equalizer, a frequent teacher, and a pleasant companion, leading me places I would never have otherwise gone. When should a man stop smoking weed? Maybe never.

I am nosing my car into a parking space in a mini–strip mall, as directed by the text message I'd received earlier, when a car pulls up behind me, blocking my retreat.

I'd taken the specified exit off the 55 Freeway in Santa Ana, California, the second-most populous city in Orange County. Erase from your internal screen for a moment the glamorous OC you see on television. This part of the province is landlocked, sunbaked, graffitied, and nearly 80 percent Hispanic; the annual per capita income is about $12,000. It is high noon. There is plenty of traffic but strangely nobody on foot. I've been here only once before, to check out the hook spot where football's fallen Robo Quarterback, Todd Marinovich, liked to score his black tar heroin, known in these parts as *chiva*, Spanish for goat.

The car behind me is low-slung and midnight blue. It idles with a throaty purr, an expensive toy that has seen better days and could certainly use a wash. I open the passenger door. Inside is a sandy-haired thirty-something; he looks like a typical marketing guy in a white dress shirt. He thanks me for driving all this way.

I get inside. He hands me a chilled bottle of Smartwater and a blindfold.

"It isn't far," he says, pulling away.

*　*　*

I smoked pot for the first time in 1968, when I was twelve years old, and smoking pot was as much of a political act as a means of getting high—I didn't even know what being *high* was about at the time, it was an abstract concept, kind of like sex. I knew it would be good, but really, I had *no idea*.

I bought my first dime bag inside a wooden stall decorated with predictable penknife etchings in the boys' bathroom on the second floor of my mid-week Hebrew school in Baltimore, Maryland. I actually talked to the guy recently on Facebook. He was considered a big stoner in those days, but now he posts endless pictures of his handsome children and adorable pugs. We had a good laugh about the bathroom stall, how far we'd both come in fifty years or so. I didn't have the heart to ask him if what he'd *actually* sold me, in a small manila envelope for ten bucks, was not weed but oregano.

At the time, I'd never been drunk, though I'd been allowed, liberally, to sip my parents' wine or scotch or crème de menthe. My parents were sober people who worked anxiously to maintain control in every aspect of life. My dad's big college drinking story involved a showdown with a rival frat president. My dad won the contest by discreetly pouring his drinks into a potted plant when nobody was looking.

For me, getting high that first time wasn't about something negative, not in the way popular culture thinks of it today. It wasn't *abuse*. It was *use*. I wasn't trying to escape my desperate circumstances. I wasn't chasing sensual or thought-expanding experiences—though that may have become more of a goal at a later date. I wasn't trying to forget my problems; I didn't really have any. And I wasn't particularly trying to rebel against my parents, who were very good to me, though rebellion was a big part of the youth culture that was reshaping the landscape all around me.

It was the time of the Tet offensive in Vietnam; it was clear the war was becoming a lost cause. The anti-war, civil rights, and women's movements had begun to roil; President Lyndon Johnson had already delivered his surrender speech to the counterculture and the coming new age, announcing that he wouldn't run for a second term. *Hey, hey, LBJ: how many kids did you kill today?* The status quo of the old white men was beginning to give way to the feelings and needs of the young, the female, those of color, and the disenfranchised.

At age twelve, deciding to smoke pot—and going to some considerable effort to find some, and to figure out how to smoke it (because that shit I got at Hebrew school definitely did not get me high at all, so I had to try several more times before succeeding in actually finding some pot)—was about two things. First, it signified I had joined the revolution my slightly older comrades, the baby boomers, had started. You grew your hair, starting with the forelock. You smoked pot. You bought your first pair of jeans, which weren't even allowed in school; in junior high we had a vitriolic protest to force the administration to legalize dungarees.

I smoked for the first time with my friend Boots Friedman and this weird kid he knew named Milton, whose parents, I could swear, were acting like Soviet spies. We sat outside behind the garage. It was summer in Baltimore, hot and sticky, the night songs of the cicadas in full chorus. I remember the sense that my perspective had changed. And that my head was floating. I felt like my face was on a balloon floating above my body, tethered by a string.

All across the country, similar initiation ceremonies were being carried out in groups of two and three, at camp sites, in basements, in Volkswagen Beetles with all the windows closed so as not to waste any smoke. "*Turn on, tune in, drop out*," advised the acid pioneer Timothy Leary at the Human Be-In, a gathering of 30,000 hippies in San Francisco's Golden Gate Park in 1967. Later it was learned that phrase had been coined for him by philosopher Marshall McLuhan, the same guy who said "the medium is the message." Whoever was responsible, we young folk were hearing loud and clear. We were being urged to detach ourselves from existing conventions. To have sex, do drugs, be free. (Birth control pills were another wonderful new drug of this era.) You have to remember, the draft was hanging over every boy's head. Each night on the news, the war came to everyone's living room. Before it was over, in 1975, some 211,000 Americans were killed or wounded in Vietnam. They were all somebody's brother, the kid from down the street. My next-door neighbor, with whom I played catch, tried to flee to Canada.

Maybe more important, at least in my own case, smoking pot was about pushing the boundaries of my sheltered suburban upbringing. With a long history of diaspora and persecution, my people, the Jews, tend to huddle together and create golden ghettos for themselves, which has worked out well in some cases but not so well in others. Moving to Pikesville, Maryland, my parents hoped to escape the persecution of their Southern upbringings. Yet, we transplanted Sagers always felt a sense of otherness, which left me with a keen feeling that there was a lot more waiting to be found somewhere, and which fostered in me, apparently, an appetite for certain brands of deviant adventure.

* * *

Any serious smoker will tell you that marijuana—besides making doughnuts taste better, movies seem cooler, and sex more intense—opens certain doors of perception. After you've smoked the first time (or five), you start seeing yourself a little differently, and this in turn makes you see the world a little differently. Maybe it makes you a little more open to things, a gateway in a positive sense.

In the course of my travels as a person and as a journalist, marijuana has served as a great equalizer, a safe and easy common denominator that has put me on the same sofa, log, or grassy knoll as people I'd never have sat down with otherwise.

You could probably substitute the words "drunk alcohol with" and come up with a pretty good story as well, though you might not remember as many of the details. But the point is this: As the ideologues of the Just Say No movement have been fond of trumpeting, marijuana has indeed been a gateway for me.

Smoking pot has opened the doors of my perception. It has led to meetings with new kinds of people outside my home community, ethnicity, religion, or economic station, people of like minds from different places. It has led me to the understanding that a person can find communality with any other human, in any setting, no matter how scary or how different they might seem.

I've smoked pot with gangbangers, actors, rap stars, construction workers, bankers, homeless guys, and millionaires. I've smoked at fourteen thousand feet in the Nepalese Himalayas with a Sherpa guide; at thirty-six thousand feet in a commercial airliner back in the days when they had smoking sections; at just below sea level on the beach of Marlon Brando's private atoll with a topless Tahitian translator; in the ruins of a factory in North Philadelphia with a bunch of thirteen-year-olds while watching pit bulls fight to the death—hey, all of those kids worked shifts selling crack and had juvie records a mile long.

I've smoked with a Bedouin and a couple of PLO operatives in a refugee camp in the Gaza Strip (we used a pipe made out of irrigation tubing); a captain of a sixty-foot catamaran in the British Virgin Islands; a dwarf in Queensland, Australia, who was once famous for being tossed; a television beauty in her Santa Monica apartment; and a pimp in a Lincoln Continental, and a hooker on a dark street corner (of course, you never smoke under the lamp). And, of course, I've smoked with Mickey Caesar, aka The Pope of Pot, a cockeyed optimist who lived his convictions even though it resulted in jail time and an early death.

I've smoked pot (and other things) with Gil Scott-Heron and Rick James. I once made Snoop Dogg cough with my own preferred strain, which I go to a lot of trouble to get. I smoked with Woody Harrelson in an underground parking lot using a health-conscientious vaporizer (plugged into a USB port in a hybrid car); as we were finishing, his friend David Blaine showed up and started doing card tricks. (Would you believe that Blaine, on regular outings, carries not just cards in his pockets but also a Sharpie to aid with tricks?) I've even smoked with my son—but only after he turned eighteen and got his own medical marijuana card.

A number of years ago, I was doing bong hits with the comedian Roseanne after an interview at her house in Lake Arrowhead, California. At one point, after staring for some time into the roaring fire in the big fireplace, she said reflectively: "All hate is just fear. All fear is insecurity."

This statement floored me, stoned or not. It seemed to sum up all the problems of humanity, the reason for wars since the dawn of time. Ethnic groups, nations, members of the various religious flocks—it is our differing forms and contents that bedevil us. What's different is always considered bad, scary, or threatening. But why? Only because it is strange to us. And we are afraid to find out more.

I haven't smoked pot with *all* the people I've interviewed. I didn't smoke with the white supremacists from the Aryan Nations, for instance, or with the high school boy from Orange County (until years later), or with Angelina Jolie—though I know a guy who used to sell pot to Brad Pitt a long time ago, when he was married to Jennifer Anniston and the couple had a quite a penchant for delivery pizza.

But I have smoked with a good many people all over the world, and it has led to a simple conclusion that has informed every bit of the work I've done as a journalist: Deep down, people are just people. We are all the same and deserve to be treated with the same respect. Angelina, the six hundred–pound man, the members of a crack gang from Venice, California, even the Nazi-worshipping miscreants from the Aryan Nations.

Drugs have given me that insight.

And I even remembered it the next day.

And all the days that followed.

Sharing a bowl with someone, you take the opportunity to share a part of yourself. Some of it is physical—you're actually sitting together with this person or persons, handing something back and forth. Some of it is neurochemistry. It's called *disinhibition*, one of the effects of THC. Given this time together with someone else, engaged in a mutual pursuit, we unconsciously suspend our disbelief. Suddenly our differences don't seem as important as our communalities. If you can share your spit on a joint, the possibilities seem limitless, wouldn't you agree?

* * *

I never set out to be a drugs correspondent.

That was the terminology used by Hunter S. Thompson, with whom I worked, at times closely, and then later succeeded in that unofficial/official position at *Rolling Stone*, and who I often think of in my own story as a personal Ghost of Christmas Future.

As I came of age as a journalist, in the late seventies and early eighties, the War on Drugs became a defining plank in the platform of our society. In a way you could say that my professional skills and my recreational expertise kind of dovetailed. I had a niche expertise.

Unlike many of the older, Ivy League Pollyannas sent by most news organizations to cover crime and drug-related stories—they seemed to mostly rely on the cops for their points of view—I had a lot of experience and insider information from the other side. By the time I got through college, I knew all about dealers and buys and stepping on shit to make more product to sell. Long before the crack epidemic, I learned how to cook freebase. Like a Harvard guy who majored in Chinese languages and became a decorated foreign correspondent, I spoke the language and customs of drugs, the dialects of the different exotic tribes within our national borders who dwelt in that world. And I was unafraid—because I already knew that people were just people, no matter how the media tried to portray them as the years went by.

As it happens, some of my fondest memories involve the subjects of these stories.

The Pope of Pot was a sweetheart, a madcap genius who called everyone *toots*. A flamboyant gay man and cockeyed optimist, he was fiercely unafraid to put his body on the line for the things he believed—and still have a good time doing it. He pissed off the cops and the New York City brass with his blatant protests and public sales of marijuana—he had the first delivery service in Manhattan and said so openly. He called marijuana "the sacrament" and considered it a holy and healing plant. He even provided his crew of bicycle messengers with a dental plan. After radio's "King of All Media" Howard Stern got wind of the Pope's operation and called him live during a broadcast, the Pope eventually went to jail, where I kept in touch via collect phone calls. Inside, he pissed blood for six months before he was allowed to see a doctor. With a fatal prognosis, the government let him go free. A few months later, he died of pancreatic cancer. He's memorialized as a character in my first novel, *Deviant Behavior*. I wonder what he would say if he knew that New York has now legalized weed, and that weed delivery is common all over the country.

In "Dab Artists," we meet some of the artisanal hash oil makers who pioneered the vape industry. A number are still my friends in person and on social media—as they prognosticated, the marijuana version of Big Pharma has become a reality, with cleaner and more sophisticated methods of production becoming the norm. Only a few of the Dab Artists I know have gone legit, many are still producing their underground product, and gatherings of Wooks at conventions around the country continue today.

Since I wrote about Dr. D., Don Davidson, a pioneer of online prescriptions in the early days of medical marijuana, he has transitioned into a successful entrepreneur, having developed a line of CBD products—the logos and packaging for which my publishing company branched out to design. His has been a wild ride through the trillion-dollar retail industry that has grown around weed and its biological sister, hemp, which is rich in CBD. Unfortunately, Dr. D. is still in court, fighting a crooked medical group that bilked him out of his first business—which specialized in THC products—and over a million dollars. Those early days in the biz were not for the faint of heart.

I have also included herein the tales of my three-week sojourn with Hunter S. Thompson. I would have several more encounters with him before he took his own life. He was kind enough to give me a blurb for my first book, *Scary Monsters and Super Freaks*. As far as I know, it was the only blurb he ever gave to another author. Of course, it took me about a hundred phone calls and faxes to finally get the blurb in hand. Many thanks to his widow, Anita Thompson, who facilitated the final, last-minute effort at press time so many years ago.

* * *

At last, the low-slung, midnight-blue sports car comes to a stop, and I am allowed to take off my blindfold, which probably hadn't looked too weird to other drivers once I'd decided to wear my sunglasses over the top.

The year is 2012. I pause a moment to assay my surroundings. I have no fucking clue where I am, other than standing outside a run-down commercial building on a lonely industrial strip. As I have so many times, I am trusting somebody to keep me safe. So far, with a few notable glitches, I have fared okay.

The inside has all the trappings of a long-abandoned building that is soon to be renovated. In one room, we find two guys, a folding table, and several bricks of a dark-green-colored marijuana concentrate—the factory and office space of a new company called DankTanks.Net. Here they are working on the very latest in marijuana technology—in the coming years, it will be widely known as vape.

If you're anything of a stoner, maybe you know that weed concentrates have become big lately—in the vernacular of the period around 2012, if a batch of concentrate was good, you'd say it was *dank*. If it was particularly good, you'd say it was *dank as fuck*, hence the name of the company. To some extent, you could say that concentrates are to marijuana as cocaine is to coca or as heroin is to opium; a substance derived from a plant though a refinement process.

To make concentrate, the trimmings from the harvest of marijuana buds (previously sold cheap) are run through machines that use butane or propane (not so healthy) or CO_2 (more organic) to distill out the active ingredients (cannabinoids and THC, the first known for their medicinal properties, the second known for getting you high). More recently, people have begun to use the buds instead; better product, better yield. At the time I visited, DankTank was fairly primitive. They used butane and the cuttings from three strong, popular strains familiar to medical marijuana patients in California: Sour Diesel, OG Kush, and Headband. The forms of concentrate differ in texture and strength depending upon the weed source and the expertise: different consistencies are called wax, butter, oil, shatter, and crumble. It's pretty easy to tell the difference by the names.

At the time, smoking concentrate could be an elaborate and ceremonial affair (as you will read in my story "Dab Artists," included herein) employing a fancy glass pipe and a blowtorch; it's called doing *dabs*. Or, more practically, you could line your weed pipe with a "green screen"—a bed of shredded weed flower, and put your dab on top of that—although this method is less efficient; often the dab is lost if not combusted at a high enough temperature.

In any case, people like concentrates for several reasons. For one, as the name says, it's a lot stronger than flower, more "concentrated." Weed usually contains up to 30 percent of the psycho-active ingredient in marijuana, THC. Concentrates can range in the mid-90s. For another reason—which will prove to be one of the keys to the popularity of vape in the future—concentrates don't smell skunky like pot. In fact, they hardly smell at all, and the vapor is more ephemeral than smoke—it dissipates quickly into the atmosphere. Concentrates, manufacturers will come to say, are stronger and more "discreet."

We sit talking as the two guys at the table—the partners in DankTanks, along with the driver of the midnight-blue sports car—melt a large, flat slice of wax into a viscus form and mix it in a glass beaker with grapeseed oil and vegetable glycerin. From there, they load syringes and inject the diluted concentrate into inch long, glass, bullet-shaped tanks. All three men are in their early thirties. Two have degrees in marketing; the third says he used to own several medical marijuana dispensaries, which were already legal in California at the time.

The third guy, who has a serious medical condition that he keeps well controlled with medical marijuana, explains his vision for DankTank. "Because you don't need any of the paraphernalia you need for smoking weed," he says, meaning grinders, lighters, ashtrays, and other smoking (and cleaning) paraphernalia, "people will be able to smoke it anywhere. Think of it. Hospitals! Assisted living facilities! Nursing homes! You just screw on the tank and hit the dank," he says with a smirk.

As he inserts his syringe into another tank to fill it up, I imagine myself in the future: an old man in a nursing home, puffing on my high-tech, electronic vape.

A harried woman in a white uniform sticks her head into the door of my room. The health care system is a mess. She has one of those nurse-caretaker personalities; she feels like the whole crumbling shebang is resting on her ample shoulders. She uses a patronizing tone: "How are we doing today, Mr. Sager?"

I'm sitting at my computer writing something. I can tell she doesn't give one shit about how I'm doing.

"Dank as fuck," I tell her with a smirk.

THE HIGH LIFE AND STRANGE TIMES OF THE POPE OF POT

A pioneer of pot delivery services, Mickey the Pope had an 800 number and a corps of bicycle messengers, all of them covered by a company dental plan. Meet the marijuana pope and his faithful followers at the Church of Realized Fantasies. Too bad the cops didn't think he was so amusing.

There's a knock at the door and Mickey the Pope, the Pope of Pot, stubs out a joint and stashes it in a drawer. "Gotta go now, toots," he rasps, smoke leaking from his chipmunk grin, and then he laughs, "Ah-ha-ha-HA!" and then he coughs, a deep black hack that shudders his shoulders. He swallows hard, wipes a tear, shrugs and smiles. A trickle of blood reddens the groove between his two front teeth.

Mickey hangs up the phone, writes a number in his little book with a green pen. His entries aren't alphabetical—more experiential, like life, taken in the order that comes, always in alternating colors. He likes things around him to be beautiful, the way God intended. He closes the book, puts a finger to his lips, concentrates. Something to do . . . What was it? . . . Hmmm. . .

Mickey pans the room, in search of a clue: refrigerator, a stack of chairs, a poster of the Italian rock and roller he has taken off the street, a hot plate with one coil glowing, his desk, a pile of bills, a birthday card. *Birthday!* Today is Mickey the Pope's birthday. He is forty-nine years old. Today is also the day before the winter solstice, the last shortening day on the calendar of seasons. This is significant somehow to Mickey the Pope, who's facing fifteen years in the slammer.

Since the bust, sales are down by more than half. Expenses, however, remain the same. It looks like Mickey will have to get a loan. He'll have to ask his little brother to cosign. His brother, of course, will insist that Mickey write something besides *pope* on the section marked EMPLOYMENT. He thinks Mickey is *meshugge*. He may be right. But the fact is, Mickey can't stop being pope just because he has no money. When you start your own church, take the top spot, register it with the City of New York, you make a lifetime commitment. You have responsibilities, toots: You have to tend the flock, buy and dispense sacrament, hire couriers—people you can trust. And then there is operations: two apartments, two offices, the church, the handouts to unfortunates, the food and the dental plan for employees, the telephone lines, 800-WANT-POT. Give the pope a call if you live in Manhattan. Leave your address, your first name, a description of yourself. Your pot will arrive by bicycle in forty minutes or less.

Mickey spies his papal miter—a high, white, John Paul crown, with underwires shaped to a peak, a nine-inch marijuana leaf pasted on the front, lace trailing from the sides. He dons it, trying the polka-dot ribbon beneath his chin. He wears the miter for all public appearances. The May Day Smoke-In at Washington Square, the Halloween parade in Greenwich Village, ACT-UP demonstrations at City Hall, Wigstock, in Tompkins Square—any occasion that requires his high-camp popely presence, any opportunity to stroll the streets, preach the gospel of marijuana, and hand out free joints, the sacrament of his Church of Realized Fantasies.

Mickey the Pope swivels around in his chair, grinning, mouth agape, glasses glinting in the fluorescent light. "Ah-ha-ha-HA!"

The door again. Knock, knock.

Oh, yeah. The door. It is made of metal. It is very heavy. Mickey shambles over and yanks. His arm boings like a rubber band. The door doesn't budge.

Mickey giggles and shrugs. What, me worry? Used to be Mickey weighed three hundred pounds. He's down a bit lately. A lot. He's a little weak. This diabetes shit. The bleeding gums, the fading eyesight. And all the time drink-and-piss, drink-and-piss, the other day he wet his pants. It was an accident. People have accidents. It'll be all right. The winter solstice is upon us, and the days will be longer, the world will be brighter. This is nature. We know this for a fact. Just as we know that when his church hits one million members, he'll have the best medical care available. Just as we know that when his case comes up, the jury will acquit. Some juror, the pope is sure, will know what he knows: that to follow an insane law is to be insane yourself.

Things may look bleak, but Mickey the Pope will find his way clear. He always has. He speaks with the voice and the authority of God. He'll tell you that himself. He also has experience on his side. Twenty years in the pot business, a dozen arrests, seven gunshot wounds, three years in various jails, one deportation, and all those men, toots, so many wonderful, beautiful men. The counselors at camp. The kids in his bunk. Ten percent of the crew of the U.S. Navy carrier *Intrepid* in the spring and summer of 1959. Two at once on public-access television, a salt-and-pepper team, the black one so big he could do it to himself if he wanted.

And then there was the guy in Amsterdam. He was hired to kill Mickey. As it was, Mickey was just wounded. Mickey was really fat then. The shot passed through the fleshy part of his right arm, down into his belly, and out again. What Mickey remembers is that oil oozed from the wounds. It looked like chicken fat, nice and bright and yellow. "I felt like an oil sheik," he says. "*Ah-ha-ha-HA!*"

In the end, the guy who tried to kill him in Amsterdam became another of the many and varied lovers of Mickey the Pope. Amsterdam: that was the place, those were the days. During the seventies, Mickey the Pope was known in Amsterdam as *Da Paus*

Maus. He was the No. 1 pot dealer in a city of heads, unloading nickels, dimes, lids, to the tune of seven kilos a day, selling out of a room in his five-story houseboat on the Amstel River, the front hatch of which was painted to resemble a giant pair of red lips. You had to come through the lips to meet the pope.

The knock again. Mickey the Pope pulls hard on the door.

Late December in the meatpacking district in New York, the sunlight leaning into the West Side afternoon. In a few hours the crack boys will stir, and the curbs will be deep in trans sex workers, and tough-looking men wearing leathers and lots of keys will come jangling down the block holding hands, headed for a basement club called the Hellfire. Now, though, things are almost serene on this corner of Thirteenth and Hudson, just in sight of the river. Mothers push strollers, delivery trucks come and go, old Irish ladies promenade—constitutionals taken daily since the boom days on the waterfront, when corners like Mickey's were given over to pubs.

The pope's place, his Church of Realized Fantasies, is painted yellow in its present incarnation, a bright beacon against dark, slick streets and dirty brick. It's an old comic book store—Dick Tracy painted on one side—with eight big windows, so good for his plants. Mickey the Pope loves plants.

Two men stand flat-footed outside the church. One wears a pompadour and a trench coat. He looks like a mobster. The other carries a pad. He looks like a balding Irish guy in a leather jacket trying to look like something other than a cop. The door swings open. "Michael Cezar?" asks the guy in the leather jacket.

"Howdy, honey, howdy!" rasps Mickey the Pope, beak nose, red faced, wearing his marijuana bonnet. He giggles, raises his hands—palms out—and rubs tiny circles in the air before him, the papal greeting.

"Internal Affairs," says the guy in the pompadour.

* * *

Back now to August, earlier in the year. Across the Americas, from Bogotá to Harlem, the drug war is raging. Though the government has proclaimed drug use is on the slide, curb-side dealers are trading briskly in cocaine, prices are down, supply stable, the rat-a-tat-tat of automatic-weapons fire rings across the ghettos like cash-register bells. Sales are also strong in heroin, an old drug making a resurgence as an antidote to crack. At first, the police notice a sudden infusion of high-grade, low-price H into the cities. Later it is revealed, but not widely reported, that most of the stuff is China White from Asia's Golden Triangle, moved into America by Triads, many of whose members have recently emigrated from Hong Kong. What fools the police is ingenuity: Chemists are processing different batches with different recipes out of the international heroin cookbook, making some of it look like Mexican, some like Lebanese.

Meanwhile, potheads across the mainland are mourning. It is the time of the drought, the great marijuana drought of 1990, the summer of scrounging, of smoking roaches and cleaning seeds, and finally, just giving up. Footage on the news shows bonfires of prime buds and old tires sending thick black smoke into the ecosystem. County sheriffs in camouflage fatigues stand around smiling, pitchforks or shotguns in hand. In the cities, the police and legislators launch a massive assault on head shops. Mail-order companies are also targeted. The police seize records, mailing lists, stock. It becomes impossible to buy a bong.

One fine summer day in the midst of all this, a New York radio personality named Howard Stern—the drive-time attitude idol of the bridge-and-tunnel crowd—is sitting at his desk at the station. He's paging through a New Jersey newspaper, looking for material for his talk show, when he spies an ad. He blinks in disbelief.

"Call 1-800-WANT-POT."

The next morning, live before 2 million listeners in three Eastern cities, Howard calls Mickey the Pope.

"Hey, dude!" Howard says. "You're on the air!"

"Howdy, honey, howdy!" rasps Mickey. "I'm the pope. The Church of Realized Fantasies."

"So what do you do, sell pot?"

"We give out sacrament for those who need it," Mickey says.

"You don't think it causes any—"

"No," interrupts the pope. "It cures everything. Even AIDS."

"It gives you breasts," blurts Howard. "How's your breasts?"

"My breath may stink a little. I didn't brush my teeth."

"No! Your breasts!"

"They're fine," says the pope. "They get erect, I suppose."

"So," says Howard, changing the subject. "You make a lot of money doing this?"

"I'm living on the Upper East Side. I'm comfy. And I have a palace in New Jersey."

"Really? All from just dealing pot?"

"Well, from being the pope. A lot of people admire the pope."

They talk a while longer, then Howard says goodbye.

"You know," Howard says to his sidekick, Robin Quivers, "I had seen the number in the newspaper, and I thought, 'This is kinda cool.' I mean, I don't think it's cool that he's a drug dealer, but it's kinda cool that he's getting away with it."

"It seems it would be pretty easy to catch him, wouldn't it?" says Robin. "You just call him up, make an order, he shows up, you book him."

"He ought to change his number to 1-800-ARREST-ME," says Howard.

* * *

Mickey the Pope was born Michael Ellis Cezar, in New York City's Greenwich Village, the eldest child of a Jewish engineer and his wife, the daughter of a former postmaster general of Jamaica who was the scion of an English colonial family that had made a fortune mining bauxite. Mickey's father owned an electronics factory in Paterson, New Jersey, which built transformers for radar, the space program, nuclear-power plants. Mickey's little brother runs the factory today. One sister is a real-estate agent; the other, a ceramics teacher who lives in the family "palace," a large house in Morris Plains, New Jersey, which has been stripped of all its furnishings to pay the family bills.

Mickey dropped out of high school after his father went bankrupt. Starting over in a new plant, Mickey built tables for machines, hooked up the electric and the plumbing, did everything from filing and drilling to sweeping the floor. Later, after a stint in the navy, he feuded with his father, who in turn disinherited his son and committed him to a mental institution. Upon his release, Mickey fled to Europe.

One day in the early seventies, Mickey took the fabled Magic Bus Tour of Amsterdam. When it stopped at the Lowlands Weed Company, says Mickey, "I knew I'd found a home."

Lowlands Weed, it turned out, was owned by a bunch of Dutch Provos, anarchists who renounced the concept of work. They were known for their be-ins, demonstrations during which they sat around and did nothing but be themselves. The Provos also advocated the legalization of marijuana. They were the original potheads of Europe, the Continent's largest dealers. They would eventually place several of their number on Amsterdam's city council. Oddly, after achieving their political foothold, the Provos disbanded. It was probably the shock. Having won, these devout anarchists found themselves in charge of legislating societal order.

"They were a bunch of crazy people," says Mickey the Pope. "This one guy threw smoke bombs at the marriage of some Dutch aristocrat. He used to have sex with women and their kids. I'm telling the truth. I had people take shits on my floor. I had other people come in and eat it.

"In the beginning, they sold pot by the plant and seeds," the pope continues. "I convinced them to sell the smokable product. Buses would pull up and three-quarters of the passengers would flow into the shop to buy pot."

Soon, *Da Paus Maus* moved out of Lowlands and founded his own retail operation, selling out of a series of ever-larger houseboats. A port city, Amsterdam had an almost inexhaustible supply of drugs. *Da Paus* would get the list of ships from the harbor master, then go down to the docks at three in the morning. He'd fall into step with some sailors, say, "Howdy, toots!" and offer to share a joint.

"And then you'd go on board and there were tons of smoke pouring out of the ship," Mickey says. "Everybody had the stuff. So I'd give them a good price and they'd throw it down on the dock, and then I'd drive out, waving to the customs guy. He knew everything. The whole government was in on it. I was once visited on my houseboat by some secretary of state. He said, 'Keep up the good work. It's great for the tourists!'"

Amsterdam had always been known for its coffee bars and hashish, but the pope saw an opening and set about creating a market for marijuana. He kept long hours, stayed open seven days a week and sold at a tiny profit—even advertised in the yellow pages as "Hennep Producten." Pretty soon, says the pope, the Cosmos, the Milky Way, Paradiso, all the big clubs were selling Mickey's finest. "I was making, like, $20,000 a day," remembers Mickey.

Mickey lived the good life for a while, spending the guilders as fast as they came in. He bought a new boat, an old schooner, to house his forty workers. He even paid for medical and dental plans. Then *Da Paus Maus* was busted. After seven years in business, Mickey was kicked out of Holland.

Penniless, still estranged from his family, Mickey landed on New York's Lower East Side in 1979. He met up with some anarchists, moved into a little apartment at First Street and First Avenue and began selling loose joints. Soon he started his first telephone delivery service, 777-CASH.

And thus began the pope's delivery empire. He serviced UN diplomats, rock stars, whorehouses, nightclubs, night watchmen, magazine editors, yippies, yuppies, and punks. For a time the pope had a diner. For a time he operated a storefront on First Street, selling bags brazenly to all comers. When that store was busted in 1981, the pope did eight months in Rikers Island Prison, whereupon he returned to the Lower East Side and started all over again, this time at Eleventh Street and Avenue B.

"People lined up outside to buy pot all day long," says a longtime associate. "They were taking the money out in garbage bags, but the cops were so busy with all the heroin in the neighborhood they didn't really have time to fool with Mickey."

The mid-eighties saw the pope battling the underworld. First came a Puerto Rican gang called the Hitmen Club. When Mickey refused to pay protection money, the gang members forced their way into his telephone center, holding the workers at bay with a .357 and a straight razor, taking $500. The next day they came back, demanding $1,000 a week from the pope. When Mickey refused, they ambushed him later on the street, shooting him six times with a .22. "He was so fat they didn't hit any vital organs," says the associate. "The ambulance guy didn't even believe Mickey had been shot until he opened up his coat and showed him the bullet holes."

Later the young sons of some Italian mobsters would try to muscle in on Mickey's operations. They cut the phone lines, waited outside to break Mickey's legs. Meanwhile, inside, Mickey the Pope was alone, in pain from a bowel obstruction, a complication from the Puerto Rican ambush. Weak, sick, determined, he held the fort for five days. In the end he was rescued by his father. "Well, I guess if you're dying, I can take you to the hospital," the old man said.

Over the years, Mickey estimates, he has presided over phone operations in more than forty different locations, always with modest success. Then came the summer of 1990, the drought. Nobody could find any pot except for Mickey. Business boomed.

Each morning, the bicycle couriers would meet at a secret location and check out stock for the day, four-gram bags of brown-green commercial Mexican, packaged in sealable glassine inside white paper envelopes. The couriers would hit the streets by 10:00 a.m. As calls came in, telephone operators would take down locations in logbooks and then beep the couriers, who would deliver the goods within forty minutes. Each bag cost the consumer $50. Delivery was $10 extra. At twenty-eight grams to the ounce, the pope's medium-grade pot was expensive, selling at about $350 a lid. But it was the only pot available. Two hundred calls a day were not unusual.

By eight each evening the couriers would check back in and pay up. No business was done after dark. That's when the real criminals were out, and couriers were often taken down by street thugs or fake cops with Chinatown shields. Mickey worried for his people. Usually, at night, the pope would gather around him a number of his flock and somebody would cook a big dinner. It was a happy family, mostly. And why not? The pope provided food, a dental plan, money to fix a broken bike. He gave out free pot, sometimes paid the medical bills of people he knew with AIDS. He'd even let you live in the telephone center or his extra apartment if you needed a place to squat. The police say Mickey was doing $40,000 a day. Mickey says he was probably making about half that much.

In any case, as quick as it came, it went. As Mickey says, "Money is like manure, toots, it's meant to be spread around."

Then, just as the church was hitting its stride, the New York police did exactly what Robin and Howard had suggested on their radio show. On September 22, 1990, the cops called the pope's 800 number. As guaranteed, a courier delivered. The police did the same again on October 12 and 26. A few days later, during the massive Halloween parade held each year in the West Village, the pope gave a joint to an undercover cop. Handing it over—as he had to so many others that evening—Mickey giggled and declared: "I'm the Pope of Pot! If you want pot, call my number!"

That was it. The NYPD labeled Mickey the Pope a high priority. "There comes a time when you have to let people know that you are serious," said Special Narcotics Prosecutor Sterling Johnson. "He defied the authorities. He threw down the gauntlet."

On November 14, with the press in tow, the cops raided the Pope of Pot. It was, said the *Village Voice*, "a police operation worthy of *America's Most Wanted*." The bust made all the news shows the next day and all the papers, even the *New York Times*. The *New York Post* played it on the front page with the headline COPS NAB PHONE 'POPE OF DOPE.' Police officials were quoted as saying that Mickey was taking 360 calls an hour on six telephones.

Mickey was brought out of his yellow church to a fusillade of flashbulbs and questions. Handcuffed, red-faced, blood pressure roaring, the pope had time to rasp only a quick, "Howdy, honey, howdy," before he was piled into a police car. Over in the shadows across the street, crack dealers and transvestites watched in amazement. They knew Mickey. On cold nights, he sometimes let them into the church to get warm. He gave out hot chocolate.

Then a cop in a suit, Assistant Chief John J. Hill, stepped forward into the klieg lights. His public statement: "We seized here a total of five messengers, two people operating the phones and the pope himself. Also seized were seven pounds of marijuana."

* * *

Nighttime now at the Church of Realized Fantasies. In an hour or two the doors will open at a club called Mars, and a benefit will commence, a bailout throw-down for Mickey the Pope. Meantime, some of the inner circle have gathered to wait. They smoke joints, watch a video of the pope, eat sponge-cake, drink hot chocolate.

Soon after his arrest and release, Mickey was arrested again, this time for participating in an ACT UP protest. Radical gays, demonstrating for a city-sponsored needle exchange for addicts, collected dirty syringes in a bucket. The pope was snatched when he attempted to turn the needles over to the police. Later he was arrested again for selling a half an ounce of pot to an undercover cop who came calling at the "palace" in New Jersey.

So it has gone. At the moment, the Pope of Pot is, to put it simply, destitute. All the change from the Mason jar in his apartment has been spent. He doesn't even have a subway token in his pocket. He has plenty of church currency—poker chips in various colors stamped in gold with his sickle and marijuana leaf insignia—but nobody wants it. MCI has cut off the 800 number; New York Tel is threatening his other accounts. Landlords are clamoring too. And, of course, there are the lawyers.

Hence the benefit, this gathering at Mickey's church. They are an odd bunch sitting on stackable plastic chairs, about two dozen of the five thousand that Mickey claims as followers, having crawled this night from the belly of an F train from the Lower East Side, descendants of William Burroughs and Alan Ginsberg and Herbert Huncke (aka Huncke the Junkie), of Madonna, Andy Warhol, and Kenny Scharf, the ever-changing members of the cult of near-fatal hipness that has thrived for so long in the East Village.

There's a guy in a Burberry raincoat, a silk tie, one eye stitched shut. A Russian Jew. A singer who is famous for looking like John Lennon. A man who looks like Charles Manson. A man named Mighty Man. One guy wears a black turban and little, square red plastic sunglasses. Another wears striped pants, a plaid coat, a Siberian fur hat. No one says a thing. Not a word. They sit, dumb, passing a joint.

Over in a corner, near the hot plate that heats the storefront, Mickey the Pope is being videoed as he watches the video of himself on a TV. An artist named Clayton has the minicam. He takes the thing everywhere, its red eye glowing, recording for a documentary that's been known for years in its many and varied forms as "the scene." Clayton made headlines in 1988 when he refused to surrender some footage to city authorities. His film showed cops, badges removed, beating homeless men and local residents with nightsticks during a riot in Tompkins Square Park. Clayton also has a storefront on the Lower East Side, on Essex below Houston, next to a kosher Chinese restaurant, in a Puerto Rican neighborhood known to Caucasian druggies from New Jersey as a good copping spot for Percodan. Clayton's mustache looks like two caterpillars inching along his lip line toward his nose. His goatee is long and thin like one of the Three Musketeers'. The hair along his two frontal lobes has been shaved. The rest hangs long in the back.

To Clayton's left is Mickey the Pope, who is being pumped by a woman for information about a friend of hers named Danny Rakowitz. Rakowitz is a Lower East Side artist and short-order cook who was arrested for cutting up his girlfriend, cooking her into soup, serving the soup to the homeless, leaving her skull and bones in a five-gallon bucket filled with Kitty Litter in the baggage claim at the bus station.

Rakowitz's friend is a tiny black woman with ashen skin and a shock of nappy hair. Her leather jacket is decorated with skull buttons. She looks like a skull, all cheekbones and sunken eyes and this thick top lip that flies up and to the left with every third word, a dancing sneer, a sort of visual "Fuck you." She is sure her friend didn't kill Monica. She's been interviewing people for months, gathering evidence. There's a plot. She knows this. Everyone is involved.

"But Danny had no reason to kill Monica," declares the skull lady. "What's the difference?" asks the pope. "The girl saw the body in the bathtub."

"Doesn't that seem strange to you?"

"Of course it does."

"Why wasn't there any blood?" asks skull lady. "Where was the blood?"

"An awful lot of cleaning, dear," says the pope, lecturing. "Put her in the tub. Cut her up. Run the water, toots. Ah-ha-ha-HA!" He raises his palms, rubs tiny circles in the air before him. "The guy is crazy. He even had a sign on the door: SOUP KITCHEN. Everybody knew it."

"Well, why didn't anybody call the cops?"

"Why didn't anyone call the cops?" repeats the pope, begging the question. He snorts and giggles. "What do you expect? It's the Lower East Side."

* * *

Only in New York, only on the Lower East Side, could somebody like the pope be the pope.

Three centuries ago, the Lower East Side was farmland and aboriginal hardwood forest, and the Bowery—now the western edge of the district, changing to Third Avenue just north of Houston Street—was a trail, used by Native Americans in their sorties against the occupying Dutch colony of New Amsterdam. Today, this jumble of factories, tenements, and storefronts, strewn from Astor Place to Alphabet City and from Fourteenth Street to Chinatown, remains the wilds of Manhattan—a campground from which the natives, with their alternative lifestyles, still launch assaults on the tastes of the mainstream uptown.

The late 1800s on the Lower East Side saw the first flowering of the immigrants. Millions of Turks, Greeks, Italians, Poles, Germans, Ukrainians, and Jews came through Ellis Island to the world's newest urban frontier. It was a dense ethnic soup, the original American pepper pot—a world, according to a WPA guidebook, "of politicians, artists, gangsters, composers, prizefighters and labor leaders."

World War II, the fifties, the early sixties, saw new waves of immigration. Jews gave way to Puerto Ricans, winos, and junkies. The Beat era was upon the East Village, a dark time of morphine, heroin, and speed, of caffeine and marijuana, of bongos, berets, turtlenecks, and homosexuality. Starting with writers William Burroughs and Herbert Huncke, poet Allen Ginsberg—continuing with Jack Kerouac, Neal Cassady, the Merry Pranksters, hallucinogens, communal living, free love—a new kind of culture, expressed in the widest range of perverse and irreverent and star-crossed possibilities, grew in the shabby far reaches of the Lower East Side.

The seventies saw the rise of the club and art scene. There were punk rockers, hip-hoppers, new wavers, performance artists, fashion designers, and drag queens. The club of the moment was CBGB; the musicians were Lou Reed, Patti Smith, Debbie Harry, the Ramones. Andy Warhol and his Factory were the spiritual center of the art world. Around him would revolve the likes of Keith Haring and Jean-Michel Basquiat.

"Although they sprang from varied backgrounds, the artists [who came to the area] shared a collective media-drenched consciousness, the heritage of the suburban teenager," writes Steven Hager in his book about the East Village. "In the sixties, this pampered upbringing was frequently a source of guilt, but in the seventies, it was dissected and rearranged, and eventually regurgitated into new forms."

In the last few years, with the fall of the economy and the rise of a new era of American Prohibition, the Lower East Side has hit hard and seamy times. "Every year it's been a different thing," says Clayton, the video artist. "Some years it's been drag queens. Other years it's been skinheads, the police, squatters, homeless. This year seems to be, you know, there's a depression happening in the country, a lot of uncertainty. They're trying to close our fire department, that's big for us. There's Mickey's bust, the Rakowitz murder,

AIDS, crack. It changes down here, but it never changes. A lot of these fuckin' people are geniuses. A lot of them are nuts."

* * *

"So what's up with the telephone center," asks the hippie. "Is it cool or not?"

"I don't know," says Mickey the Pope.

"Well, we're only doing twenty deliveries a day, and that ain't shit!"

"Put me on PR!" chimes in Bartman. "Give me a minimum budget! Give me no budget!"

The pope eyes Bartman, shakes his head in sorrow. Bartman, Freddie Redpants, Larry the Libertarian . . . why can't he find some help? Why must he do everything himself? Here in the church, a few days before his birthday, Mickey the Pope is in ruins. The other night at the fundraiser at Mars, seven hundred people crowded all four floors. It was a raging success. There was so much support for the pope that you couldn't move across the room. Unfortunately, nobody at the benefit thought about collecting any money.

In the end, Mickey the Pope lost forty dollars.

So now he has gotten himself a new partner. Call him the hippie. He is bald on top with a fringe of shoulder-length hair, a gray beard cascading down his chest. He is hyper, creepy. He keeps looking all around him. Toward the windows. The back room. Under the papers on Mickey's desk. "So what about the phone center?" he asks again, picking up the trash can, checking the bottom, putting it back down. "Is it cool?"

"Well, there wasn't a big investigation," interrupts Bartman. "They didn't freeze his bank accounts. It was just—"

"Baaaaaaart!" chides the pope.

"Listen, you little turd!" says the hippie, eyes suddenly wild, finger in Bartman's nose. "What you gotta do is one thing. Meet Red each morning, pick up, work. No talking. Got it?"

"I've cut back about twenty percent," says Bartman. "I'm definitely talking less. I'm gonna—"

"You're gonna do what you got to do!" hollers the hippie, puffing up, ballistic, a vein popping in his right temple. He zeros in on the hapless Bartman: "Look. I got a lot going for me right now. I can't have some little pussy to fuck it up. If I'm gonna go to jail for conspiracy, I'll kill a fucker and go to jail for the same amount of time!"

"I'm with that!" says Bartman.

"You know what I'm sayin'?" asks the hippie.

"Fuck! I swear!"

"Now, now, boys, boys," says the pope, batting his eyelashes, an aging coquette with curly gray beard. "This is the sacrament we're talking about Please. . . . Respect. *Ah-ha-ha-HA!*"

* * *

The pope is at home now, his Upper East Side studio, a second-floor walkup. He's not feeling too well, lying shirtless on his unmade bed amid a clutter of plants and clothes and videos with titles like *Hot Rocks II*, his scars and bullet wounds looking pink and ropy amid the forest of fine graying hairs covering his torso.

Over in the kitchen, a friend of the pope's is scouring the oven. The sink is filled with dishes. A flesh-colored marital aid pokes up out of the soapsuds. The friend has just been released after twenty years in prison. He doesn't want his name mentioned, but he intimates that he had something to do with an art heist and a murder at a big museum in New York City. He met the pope in prison. All the Jewish guys there knew each other. He looked out for the pope. They also took ceramics together. The pope is letting him crash in a basement apartment while he looks for a job in his old field, public relations.

It is time now for a papal audience. Why? The pope is asked. Why is he setting up business anew? Why is he letting a reporter see all this? Does he have to have an 800 number? Couldn't he just chill like the other eleven delivery services in Manhattan, do a thriving underground business? Perhaps Howard Stern is right. Is he begging to go to jail?

"I'm the bringer of wisdom and truth," explains Mickey the Pope. "I'm doing what's right. I'm the kind of person, you're not gonna intimidate me. Marijuana is the saving plant. It should be legal. People want it that way. The voice of the people is the voice of God in a democracy. If you get enough people into it, the politicians have to listen. I think what we should do is, sort of set up our own society and do our own thing. Let all the others go do what they will. We're doing what's right and proper and screw 'em, our little group should live better than they do. We should win by example."

With that the tape recorder clicks off. The pope takes a long slow drink from a gallon jug of water, then grins, bats his lashes. "So how'd I do, toots?" he asks. "This is serious. I don't want to go to jail. I really don't want to go to jail."

* * *

Now it is Mickey the Pope's birthday, the day before the winter solstice, the last shortening day on the calendar of the seasons. There's a knock at the church door, and Mickey opens up and finds two undercover cops. One wears a pompadour and a trench coat. The other carries a pad.

"Oh! Internal Affairs!" giggles Mickey the Pope. "I called you, didn't I?"

"Yes, sir," says the cop with the pad. He regards Mickey for a moment, beak nosed, red faced, wearing his marijuana bonnet. The cop rolls his eyes to the heavens. "Mind if we come in?"

"Of course, toots," rasps the pope, bowing, gesturing, showing the guests to some chairs.

"So what happened?" asks the cop with the pad.

"Well, when I was busted, there was this big media thing, you know, and John J. Hill said there were seven pounds confiscated in the raid."

"John J. Hill?" asks the pad.

"Yeah, he's an assistant chief."

"Oh! Chief Hill!" exclaims the pompadour, leaning forward.

"He said there were seven pounds?" asks the pad.

"Right there on the news," says Mickey.

"Oh," says the pompadour.

"So how many pounds were there?" asks the pad.

"Close to five."

"So, close to five pounds were taken into evidence by the police?"

"Right," says the pope.

"So, what's the problem?" asks the pompadour.

"Well, I was only indicted for two- and one-half pounds."

"So what's the problem?" asks the pad.

"See," says the pope, grinning. "Two- and one-half pounds are missing! Cops shouldn't be stealing the evidence. I mean, I don't steal. I don't jump turnstiles, none of that shit. I really don't. I live the pure life. I don't take from nobody, and that's the truth."

"I see," says the pompadour.

"The thing is, if the cops want pot, they should have to buy it like everyone else," says the pope. "If you're not gonna charge me for it. I want it back. After all, it's the sacrament. This is the church. The marijuana church. The Church of Realized Fantasies."

DAB ARTISTS

In the early years of legal marijuana, the craftsmen on the outlaw edge of the vaping boom worked in the shadows. They called themselves "Wooks." They extracted only the finest erl, crumble, and shatter, strictly gourmet. Cool but nerdy, deliberately unkempt, more comfortable alone or in small groups, these self-taught Heisenbergs of hash oil convened once a year for the Secret Cup Finals in Las Vegas. A look at the last days before the machinery of legalization took hold.

We were somewhere around Barstow, on the edge of the desert in a driving rain, when my passenger, James "Skywalker" Johnson, began to fidget with the well-traveled, antiballistic, Pelican-brand polypropylene case resting on the floor mat between his feet. Hazard yellow and covered with stickers, equipped with double-throw latches and a heavy-duty handle, it resembled something the modern army might carry into battle, a safe box for a delicate gun sight or high-end piece of electronics.

Skywalker is a chunky man of thirty-two with a burner cell phone, an exceptionally well-developed palate, and a bit of an asthmatic wheeze. A former intern for a Republican US senator—his season in Washington politics left him sprinting for the exit—he has worked as a bartender, a chef, a computer programmer, and a marijuana grower. Now, he says, he's "an ambassador for a California-based lifestyle brand inspired by the culture of hash oil." As such, he buys and sells marijuana buds and trim, hash oil and edibles, T-shirts and hats. He'd tell you more, but many of his activities are illegal, even though his products are not. His and the names of many other individuals and companies in this story have been changed.

On a stormy December afternoon, we were headed to Las Vegas for the fourth annual Secret Cup Finals, the culmination of a yearlong series of regional judged events that bring together the best artisanal hash-oil makers in the country. The festivities were to be held in a rented mansion off the Strip. Skywalker had paid dearly for a room in a guesthouse by the pool. His fledgling concern, Jedi Extracts, was one of the sponsors. Besides looking forward to representing his brand, making new contacts, and sampling all the entries—some of which for sure would be "fire," meaning the best of the best—Skywalker was stoked to meet up again with his friends in the elite community that has grown up over the past half-decade around the business and craft of making hash oil, called extraction.

Cool but nerdy, deliberately unkempt, more comfortable alone or in small groups, these self-taught Heisenbergs of hash oil call themselves "Wooks," after the fierce but cuddly Star Wars creatures many of them resemble. Mostly men in their twenties and thirties, they favor beards and tats, blown-glass pendants, food-stained hoodies, and flat-brimmed ball caps with collectible pins decorating the crowns. Known by their colorful handles—Big D, Brutal Bee, Task Rok, Witsofire, the Medi Brothers, Hector from SmellslikeOG—the Wooks devote their lives to producing and smoking the very finest hash oil, a form of concentrated marijuana that can be extracted from the leaves and flowers of the pot plant by a variety of chemical processes, the most common of which employs ordinary cans of highly volatile butane lighter fluid as a chemical solvent.

Hash oil (the formal name is butane hash oil, known as BHO) is a modern version of hashish. The butane gas and lab equipment replace the intensive labor of patting, sifting, and compressing marijuana flowers that go into the traditional method of creating hash. Since the 1960s, devotees have been making a sludgy form of hash oil, usually on the stove in a pot using a variety of toxic solvents including naphtha, hexane, or isopropyl alcohol. A precursor to BHO began to appear around 2000 in Los Angeles's San Fernando Valley. The first recognized iteration was called Juice. It was smoked primarily on top of a green screen—a pipe bowl full of pot or pot ash. Some preferred to chase the dragon, using a straw and a hot knife or a piece of foil and a flame.

Almost from the beginning, enthusiasts started making their own pipes. Soon the glass blowers became involved; today you can buy elaborate blown-glass pipes that cost tens of thousands. When smoked, hash oil produces a more substantial rush than marijuana flowers, but the overall high doesn't last as long. A heavy smoke session often leads to a spontaneous nap. The Wooks call this condition DTFO, Dabbed the Fuck Out. They take great sport in posting DTFO photos of one another on social media.

BHO was first widely publicized in 2009, when it won "best product" at the *High Times* Cannabis Cup in Amsterdam. The founders of the Secret Cup, Jeremy Norrie and Daniel de Sailles, were part of the team that first brought hash oil to the Amsterdam competition. According to many but not all, they helped popularize the term dab, which was coined to describe the approximate dosage. ("Dabbing" means smoking hash oil.)

Like pot, hash oil can be purchased legally in a dispensary or illegally from an extractor or a dealer. The categories of hash oil vividly denote the different textures of the stuff, which originates as a liquid but eventually hardens into a solid state unless otherwise prepared. There is wax, shatter (as in broken glass), budda (butter), honeycomb, live resin (sticky), crumble (like crack), and honey oil. Hash oil of a lesser grade and potency is also used for edibles, tinctures, lotions, drinks, and e-vape cartridges.

The colors range from vivid greens to golden yellows to burnt-sugar browns. A translucent golden amber is considered the connoisseur's choice. As a rule, Skywalker will not smoke anything that's not clear, even some of the Secret Cup entries. "I'm not putting that shit in my lungs," he often says, implying that he doesn't know who'd extracted it or how.

At this writing, twenty-three states and the District of Columbia allow some form of legal marijuana use, medical or recreational.

Twelve states explicitly allow for the use of marijuana extracts, which lack the telltale skunky smell of marijuana—the buzzword in the industry is *discreet*. However, only two states permit extraction, Colorado and Washington, where rigorous laboratory specifications must be met. "In the other ten states," says Paul Armentano of the National Organization for the Reform of Marijuana Laws, "arguably the extracts are legal when they fall from the sky."

Today, as large companies and venture capitalists rush into the rapidly expanding hash-oil arena, Skywalker and his fellow Wooks are fighting for their piece of the future. Echoing the sentiments of artisanal craftsmen in other fields, they are hoping that quality and discriminating palates win the day—or at least keep them in business as the giants grab bigger shares of the market.

For the Wooks, attending the Secret Cup is like attending a high-level trade show. (For legal reasons, the finals are considered a private party.) It's sort of a March Madness for extractors—not the only such contest in the world, but maybe the most exclusive. The regional winners were going to be present at the finals as well as some of the winners from the previous year. In all there would be twenty entrants. Bragging rights and future contracts were at stake. If Skywalker and the others want to compete in their rapidly growing field, they need to be known, to be intimate with the doings and players in their industry, to cultivate an aura of insider success.

But it won't be just work. It is, after all, Las Vegas. These Secret Cup gatherings have become somewhat dear to Skywalker. Wooks are loners. Their lives are furtive and solitary. Most reside in rural areas in states where they could easily be busted. If they are busted—as was a friend of Skywalker's who blew up a house when the butane exploded—none of the other Wooks will dare to call, fearing their friend's communications are being monitored by police. As it is, their community exists mostly on social media. Attending the Secret Cup would be some of Skywalker's best friends, the people with whom he Facebooks and Instagrams regularly. Hanging out for five days in Vegas with his fellow Wooks, eating, smoking, wreaking a little havoc on the Strip—"What's not to like?" Skywalker said in his gruff East Coast manner.

By three in the afternoon the storm was still raging, and we had two hours left to drive. The desert sky was black. Gusting winds buffeted the car. As we made our way toward Las Vegas, the red lights in front of me were a watery mirage. Skywalker was biting his pinkie fingernail, a nervous tell I'd begun to notice during our time together. At some point, I heard a deep sigh emanating from his vicinity, followed by a rattling cough. Out of the corner of my eye I noticed him reach down between his feet, throw the double latches of his Pelican case.

From the custom foam padding arranged inside, he withdrew his Mini Sundae Cup rig. Five inches tall, made of clear glass by a company called Hitman, the pipe retails for $500 and uses a small amount of water as a filter. The bowl on top, called a nail, is an after-market add-on, fabricated of the finest quartz. (Some enthusiasts prefer nails made of Grade 2 titanium, a type used in missiles.) Placing the rig in the cup holder, Skywalker reached into his backpack and removed a bottle of water, a small paper bindle of hash oil, and a butane torch.

The torch was bigger than a cigar lighter but smaller than a Bunsen burner. He pulled the trigger, a loud click like a gun dry firing. A four-inch cone of orange-blue flame burned briefly, illuminating the inside of my car.

"Mind if I do a dab?"

* * *

Two months earlier. October in central Phoenix.

A couple dozen white canopy tents, arranged roughly in a circle, baked in the sun like so many covered wagons on an asphalt prairie. Plumes of light smoke rose here and there, mixing in the enervated air with the smell of hot dogs from the vendors by the gate.

The Secret Cup Desert Regional was the sixth stop on the 2014 Secret Cup circuit. Like all the others except the final, it featured a weekend expo open to the public. The Secret Cup could be called a smaller, more specialized version of the huge gatherings made popular over the years by *High Times's* Cannabis Cups. A cross between a farmers' market and a renaissance fair, the expo is a pop-up festival for connoisseurs of artisanal hash oil, edibles, and other concentrates. Available for sale alongside various marijuana products were paraphernalia, art, and clothing. In one area, glass blowers demonstrated their skills. For the price of admission—$20 per day—anyone who presented a medical marijuana license could smoke as many dabs as they were able. There were also deals to be had: A gram of top-shelf hash oil was selling for as little as $50, about half the going rate in dispensaries.

Beneath one of the white tents, in a booth rented by Jedi Extracts, Skywalker and his right-hand man, a guy called the Captain, were working the crowd with the zeal of boardwalk hucksters, pushing a drinkable hash-oil extract. Suspended in cherry syrup, it is sold in a small red pharmaceutical bottle to resemble the narcotic cough medicine known in hip-hop circles as Purple Drank, a combination of promethazine and codeine. You might call it a novelty item, but it has a pleasing taste and a copacetic effect, especially over ice in the heat. Sales were brisk.

Seated alongside Skywalker and the Captain at a folding table was an extractor named Sloth Bear, one of several with whom Skywalker works. By necessity there's a lot of collaboration in the hash-oil trade. Skywalker neither grows pot nor extracts oil, though he has done both. These days, he finds the weed. He finds the extractors. He finds the producers of hash-oil capsules or gummy bears or syrup. He finds the dispensaries to take these items off his hands. Each deal is different, but the best scenario for Skywalker is when dispensaries provide all the marijuana and Skywalker takes it to someone like Sloth Bear, who extracts the oil. Skywalker and his extractor usually take a 50 percent cut; often they consign their product back to the dispensaries for sale. Skywalker is essentially a middleman. His talent is knowing the right people and finding the right pot, making deals happen, opening territories.

Sloth Bear, who is twenty-nine, has an entry in the Desert Regional this weekend. He's well-known in Wook circles; in the past, he placed in the top four in the hash-oil division of a *High Times* Cannabis Cup. On the table in front of Sloth Bear was a large slab of fresh oil, gold tinged with green, a pungent form called live resin that's made with fresh frozen buds. Also on the table, along with the bottles of syrup and cans of soda mixer, were a couple of dab rigs and a butane torch.

Like many of the booths at the Desert Cup expo, Jedi Extracts was giving away free dabs. A double line of customers trailed ten deep into the brutal sun, waiting to taste and buy. They reflected a cross-section of who is interested in dabbing erl, Wook slang for hash oil. A father and son looking like they made a wrong turn on the way to a Lions Club picnic. A graying hippie with a pendant pipe around his neck. A withered man in an electric wheelchair. A fiftyish woman wrapped head to toe in diaphanous scarves. A pair of Suicide Girls with extensive facial piercings. A pair of high school boys trying to look like they belonged.

"Step right up," called Skywalker, pocketing the proceeds of another sale. "Who needs a free dab? Who wants a pour?"

Born in Queens, Skywalker moved to rural Pennsylvania at an early age. His father was a service manager for a car dealership, his mother worked for a logistics firm. High school in the middle of nowhere was an invitation for hijinks. "Because we were so bored, whenever some little thing popped off," Skywalker said, "we would go hard at it and just be assholes." He and his friends would drive down roads taking out mailboxes with baseball bats, hang out at the houses of people who weren't home, heckle the police, smoke as much weed as they could find.

Skywalker dropped out of tenth grade and went to work for a local newspaper, where his facility with computers and message boards became prized. After getting his GED, he paid his own way through college. From there he drifted around the country, trying various trades. Then he fell into the medical marijuana business and things just clicked. He ran a grow in the Northeast for four years; later he taught himself extraction. In 2011, seeing an opportunity to expand, he moved to California and started Jedi Extracts.

As the day wore on, the temperature continued to rise. Heat eddied off the pavement but the customers kept coming; Skywalker and the Captain kept pouring Styrofoam cups, $10 for a one-ounce drank with soda, $35 for a four-ounce bottle. Meanwhile, Sloth Bear had brought out another slab. Under arrangement with Skywalker, he was selling (and giving away) his own stuff. Already he'd made back his expenses. Sloth Bear and Skywalker agree it's cool to travel around the country meeting up with your fellow Wooks and furthering your craft and your business. But it's quite another thing to pay for all that travel and feed yourself. Accordingly, spirits inside the booth this afternoon were high, despite the wilting temperatures.

"I wish I'd brought another case of syrup," Skywalker said, looking through the empty boxes at his feet. He would not reveal the source of the syrup or the arrangements under which he was selling it. Like any entrepreneur, however, he basically has three goals at the various Secret Cup expos and gatherings: To make his brand ever more prominent. To continue to make new friends and visit with established ones, opening up lines of commerce and goodwill. To make enough money to continue to operate.

"Gimme two more bottles," said a returning customer, a tall black man with dreads.

"That's what's *up*," enthused the Captain, taking four twenties and making change. The Captain brings to mind Turtle from *Entourage*. A couple of years ago, when he met Skywalker, he was working as a janitor in a fast-food restaurant. Now they're roommates.

"Mind mixing me a drank?" Sloth Bear asked, weighing out another gram of his live resin on a small electronic scale. A bead of sweat broke free from his thick hairline and slid down his temple.

"Only if you give me a dab," the Captain said.

"All you need do is ask, my good man," said Sloth Bear.

Born and raised in Southern California, Sloth Bear is the son of a contractor and a chiropractor. In high school, he was busted with two pounds of weed. Three months before his probation was to end, he rear-ended an elderly lady and was charged with DUI. He turned twenty-four in jail. "It was the worst birthday ever," he said.

After working in a movie theater and then in construction with his dad, Sloth Bear was hired at a hydroponics store. Over four years, Sloth Bear—who is large and furry but not slothful—worked as a manager. Meanwhile, he learned hydroponic growing from his boss, a farmer of legal crops, and from his customers, many of whom cultivated pot. Sloth Bear started growing for others and eventually discovered his aptitude for extracting. At one of the competitions, he met Skywalker and the Captain. They became fast friends and co-conspirators in a criminal enterprise that somehow never feels criminal to them. It might be hard and stressful, but at the end of the day, over a number of dabs, each of them will tell you, as Sloth Bear said: "It's what I was born to do."

Now, under the white canopy tent, Skywalker grabbed one of the rigs from the folding table and pointed to a dab that Sloth Bear had just prepared for the frat boy standing in front of the folding table. "I'm ready for another dab."

"*That's* what's up," said Sloth Bear.

Everybody laughed.

* * *

Early November in the high desert in California. Harvest season at Merlin's MediFarm.

According to the ten-day forecast, a storm was headed toward us. Rain on the plants at this point could wreck the buds. All around the farm, everyone worked with a sense of urgency. A pair of men used a pulley to haul pot from the lower terraces. Inside the curing shed, three laborers hung buds on hundreds of lines to dry. On the porch of the house a woman sorted seeds. Sloth Bear was beneath a shade tent, preparing to blast his next batch.

Making hash oil is an ever-evolving art. Every extractor working today learned his or her craft largely from YouTube, chat rooms, social media, and trial and error. Some extractors choose to leave the buds on the plant longer, some want an earlier harvest. Some prefer the buds, called nugs, to be dried for up to ten days. Some deep-freeze immediately. There is no particular consensus on which method is best. Each strain produces a different result, which is the essence of artisanal erl. As with wine or cheese or beer, there is creative variance between products, a diverse palette of smells and tastes and effects.

Marijuana has two major active ingredients. Tetrahydrocannabinol (THC) causes people to feel energetically inspired. Cannabidiol (CBD) relieves pain and a number of medical conditions, from glaucoma and seizures to arthritis and anxiety. Pot is also rich in terpenes and terpinoids, aromatic hydrocarbons produced by plants to deter herbivores. Hash oil can smell like tangerine, lemon, grapey purple perfume, pine, earth, or cherry candy.

Merlin's MediFarm grows sixty-three different strains, among them standards like Chemdawg, Girl Scout Cookies, and Sour Diesel. Sloth Bear has a contract this year to convert about three-fourths of the farm's two hundred to four hundred pounds of crop into hash oil. Sloth Bear supplies the butane and the equipment; in return he receives 50 percent of the oil produced, with an option to sell it back to the grower.

Depending upon the strain and the method of growing—and the techniques, tools, and prowess of the extractor—a pound of marijuana will yield anywhere from 30 to 120 grams of oil. The oil will sell wholesale to dispensaries from $20 to $40 a gram and to buyers for between $80 and $100. (For comparison, flower marijuana sells retail from $10 to $20 a gram in dispensaries.)

BHO extractors use one of two types of equipment to make hash oil, either an open-loop or a closed-loop system. For this batch, Sloth Bear employed a SubZero Scientific brand open-loop extractor with tripod legs that he bought used for $400. It fits easily into his vehicle along with the rest of his equipment: a couple of medium-size plastic propagation trays (usually for growing seeds or clones); two Pyrex baking dishes; a supply of parchment paper; a two-inch hose clamp; and a couple of round filters (one paper, one silk) to place at the bottom of the cylinder.

Now, under the shade tent—which allowed for plenty of ventilation—Sloth Bear introduced the nozzle of a large can of refrigerated butane into a receptacle at the top of the SubZero Scientific extractor, which at the moment contained a quarter pound of a strain called Sour Maui Dawg.

As we sat on beach chairs behind a folding table, the liquid butane passed under pressure through the bud-packed metal cylinder, dissolving the crystallized resins in the marijuana flowers, including the THC, CBD, terpenes, flavonoids, and also something called myrcene, one of the primary components of hops, which is partly responsible for the sedative effects of beer. In a few moments, a viscous stream of clear amber oil began to flow. The oil landed atop the organic parchment paper, which was folded to form its own tray within the Pyrex dish, which itself sat in a warm bath of one hundred–degree water in the propagation tray.

Pleased with himself, Sloth Bear gestured toward the healthy flow of golden oil. "I always wanted to make a million before I was thirty," he said.

By the time this harvest was through, he said, he'd be halfway there.

* * *

December again. The Secret Cup Finals in Las Vegas.

By late Saturday afternoon a cloud of smoke, cookout grease, and man funk hung over all the rooms of the rented mansion. Beneath the thunder of the DJ's rap music could be heard the soundtrack of serious dabbing—the mini-jet-engine whoosh of butane torches, the gurgle of percolating bubbles, the continuous series of barking coughs emanating from here and there like the croaking calls of frogs in a wetland.

The venue, as advertised, was enormous. To one side of the foyer, with its winding staircase and crowning chandelier, was a grand dining room. Under a hand-painted ceiling, the chairs were filled with Wooks. Everyone had a Pelican case. The long table was littered with pipes and bindles and dead cans of 'tane. Many had brought their electric nail, a bowl wired to a heating element to maintain a constant temperature, keeping the pipe ever ready to melt the next hit. Thinking ahead, some even brought extension cords.

On the other side of the foyer was a sitting room. Like much of the house, it was decorated with faux-gold Versace furniture. A faux-gold-plated custom motorcycle occupied a velvet-covered platform in the bay window.

Skywalker was arranged on a gold fainting couch, his eyes at half-mast. The room he'd anted up for had turned out to be a tiny, converted cabana. During the storm, which lasted several days, there was a nasty leak. He hadn't gotten much sleep.

Sitting opposite Skywalker in a Louis XIV knockoff was a Wook named Gerald, from Boston. The two first met at the Secret Cup's Beast Coast Regional in Providence, Rhode Island. Since then, they've collaborated on some deals. They were supposed to be sharing the full-size bed in the wet cabana; mostly they had powered through the gathering without sleep. Their rigs and torches were arranged haphazardly on a coffee table between them. Nearby, on another gold chair, was a VIP guest—one of one hundred people who'd paid $300 to $500 (depending upon the quality of the gift package included) to be allowed to attend the mansion between 3 and 11 p.m., smoke free samples of the entries, and rub elbows with the finalists. The VIP's glass pipe was also on the table. A pricey piece, it was artfully blown to resemble a dead infant with a bloody amputated leg.

Gerald is twenty-one. He calls his company Southie Extracts. Like many of the other Wooks, he started extracting because he liked erl but couldn't find any. Last April, at the Beast Coast Regional, he was one of the finalists. "I never really thought I'd win," he said. "I just did it for fun."

"Did you try number seventeen? That's the winner right there," Skywalker said with his usual confidence. "It's the Samurai Bros entry."

"How do you know it's the Samurai Bros?" Gerald challenged. The entries wouldn't be unmasked until the scores were tabulated Sunday afternoon.

"I've bought three or four grams of that shit," Skywalker said dismissively. With a lot of the West Coast guys, he's found, you can't do much arguing; they're too mellow. But guys from the East Coast like him and Gerald see arguing as sport. Sometimes he misses that. "Don't you smell that fuckin' tang?"

Gerald dipped into his judge's pack, a leather-covered jeweler's box with foam spaces for twenty small glass jars, each one numbered. As a Secret Cup finalist, he was charged with tasting and grading his competitors. He selected number seventeen.

Twisting open the top of the jar, Gerald retrieved a small folded-up square of nonstick parchment paper, the same as Sloth Bear uses. (Having failed to make the top four at the Desert Regional, Sloth Bear was off in Hawaii with his girlfriend, following the proceedings online.)

Gerald unfolded the bindle once and then again. Between his fingers was something that appeared to be a small, thin, translucent piece of used chewing gum pressed between the sheets of the paper. Gerald pulled apart the halves with a precise movement, bringing to mind Velcro and causing a similar sound. What confronted him at last was a half-gram of shatter—think of a small piece of amber glass you might find on a beach.

Gerald brought the sample to his nose with the practiced air of an oenophile or foodie. "This smells like tangie," he said, meaning tangerine.

"It's grapefruity," Skywalker corrected. "I definitely get more of a grapefruit."

"It looks flame," said Gerald.

"It *is* flame," assured Skywalker, folding his arms like, *Told you so, dude.*

Gerald triggered a large butane torch and proceeded to heat the Halen Honey Hole of Skywalker's Mini Sundae Cup rig.

As he aimed the orange-and-blue cone of fire toward the bowl, I asked if they ever worried about going to jail. After all, their passion and livelihood is illegal in all but two states, and neither lives in one.

"I do think about the legal aspects, but you can't really worry about it," Gerald said. Heating a nail can take up to thirty seconds, depending how much fun the user is having, or how mesmerized he gets, or how much residual oil needs to be cooked off. "I am a big believer in karma," he said, "so I feel like if you live a good life and you're a good person then bad things don't happen to you."

"Extraction is going to be legal eventually," Skywalker said. "More sooner than later. To be involved in the community now means we'll have that first jump in our own states when big business comes in with their millions and millions of dollars. That's why I feel good to be at the Secret Cup. It makes you feel like you've made it a little bit. The people here are the major players."

Gerald continued to heat the nail until the quartz glowed red, then removed the flame and set the torch on the table. He tested the temperature of the nail by holding it near the underside of his wrist, the place where a father might test a few drops of baby formula.

At last he applied the four-inch titanium dabber to the inside of the heated bowl. At the end of the dabber was a glob of the entry in question. Immediately upon contact with the hot quartz, the dab liquefied, then bubbled, then vaporized. A light white smoke traveled through the chambers, spinning a tiny glass propeller. At the other end of the dabber was a cup called a carburetor cap. Gerald placed the cap over the nail to trap the smoke as he continued to inhale. When he finished the hit, Gerald put down the rig, inclined his chin, and exhaled a thick stream of smoke toward the chandelier.

He noted an immediate increase in his energy level, a cerebral sensation of floating, a tingle at the top of his head. His eyes felt recessed, his point of view at once more internalized and more externalized, everything more vivid and intense. The music washed pleasantly into his ears, into his brain, something hypnotic by Kendrick Lamar: *Bitch, don't kill my vibe. Bitch, don't kill my vibe.*

"That *is* flame," Gerald said at last, eyes wide. He looked over to Skywalker for concurrence.

Homie was DTFO.

* * *

January in downtown Denver.

I followed Ralph Morgan, the chief executive officer of two related but independent companies, Organa Labs and O.penVAPE, through the front door of a nondescript brick industrial building. Morgan, who is forty-two, was dressed in Rocky Mountain casual. We'd just finished lunch at his favorite sushi place. Before he got into the pot business, he sold replacement joints, primarily knees and hips. His wife, Heidi, sold pharmaceuticals. "We were totally naïve to cannabis," he said. "We saw the push for legalization in Colorado on the news and were intrigued. As soon as we started doing our due diligence, we fell in love with the idea. I used to tell people, 'Hey, we've been selling joints and drugs for years, so we're qualified!'"

The Morgans opened Evergreen Apothecary in 2009. It is located on South Broadway, in an area called the Green Mile, an up-and-coming neighborhood with one of the highest concentrations of dispensaries in the world. The business took off. But Morgan was unhappy with the inconsistency of his products. "We were telling patients, 'Hey, eat this brownie, but just a quarter of it—hopefully that's the same strength as the last time.'" Morgan said. "If this is medicine, shouldn't a doctor be able to prescribe a specific type and dosage? We were looking for something that could be reliable and reproducible."

The Morgans opened Organa Labs in 2010 and O.penVAPE in 2012, the latter in partnership with a chain of dispensaries. For tax reasons, the two companies are separate. O.penVAPE, which makes several different models of battery-powered portable vaporizers, or e-vapes, does not touch marijuana, so it is not subject to the higher taxes on pot-related industry. Organa does all of the extracting. Financial analysts say it is conceivable the combined companies will be worth a billion dollars in two years.

Morgan led me into a laboratory full of gleaming stainless-steel machines and tanks. Dials, hoses, knobs, and wires were everywhere. From floor to ceiling, everything looked spotless. In front of me stood three Supercritical Fluid Extraction Systems manufactured by the Waters Corporation. Equipped with a computer interface and CO_2 recycle options, capable of extracting at pressures of 5,000 psi, the machines cost about $165,000 each.

Organa makes hash oil using a process called supercritical CO_2 extraction, the same technique for decaffeinating coffee and drawing essential oils from rose petals for perfume. Supercritical CO_2 is an organic compound that exhibits properties of a gas as well as a liquid. Because of this, the CO_2 is able to flow through the chopped marijuana as a gas would, but it also acts like a solvent, as a liquid would, pulling out the desired molecules of THC and the rest. To achieve this supercritical state, great amounts of pressure are needed, one reason the machines are so expensive.

By growing its own pot, Organa can make hash-oil products with consistent standards and strengths. Its hash-oil cartridges are designed to be used with O.penVAPE's electronic vaporizers but can be used with others as well. According to the company, it is selling cartridges at a rate of one every ten seconds, more than 250,000 per month. To keep up with demand, Organa has about ninety thousand square feet of indoor grow space in Colorado. It has recently bought a three hundred–acre ranch in Pueblo; city and banking officials are working with the company, because they believe it will bring jobs and commerce.

Among Organa Labs' most intriguing products are CannaTabs, small tablets designed to dissolve under the tongue. The tabs are sold in pill bottles, twenty-five milligrams per tab, and are available in several forms, including sativa, indica, and a hybrid. Sativa has a lot of THC, for an "up" feeling. Indica has a lot of CBD for sleep aid and pain relief. Patients can feel effects in as little as ten minutes, as opposed to thirty to forty-five for edibles.

"Our target market is a lot of people who haven't tried marijuana in twenty years, and now that it's in this really convenient dosage, they're willing to try it," Morgan said, leading me through the facility. In one area sat large industrial vacuum ovens. In another, women with surgical masks and gloves used syringes to fill cartridges with hash oil.

Going through Organa's extensively inspected, medical-grade lab—where, according to law, every batch of pot gets tested for strength and is given a bar code that follows it from field to dispensary—I couldn't help but think about all the Wooks I'd met over the preceding six months. Working as fast as possible, Sloth Bear can blast three pounds a day with his single-loop extractor. Organa's three CO_2 extractors can blast between sixty and one hundred pounds a day; the company has recently purchased an extractor that can process ten times faster. As more and more states pass their own medical or recreational marijuana laws, companies like Organa—with millions in capital at their disposal—are poised to move into the market and dominate.

Skywalker and his fellows will likely never become giant players like Morgan. But it's also hard to envision a world where creativity, enthusiasm, and refined craft are trampled into dust. We live in an age of multiple choices. We can choose processed cheese or something funky from France. Wine in a box or wine from Italy. Hash-oil tablets from Organa or shatter from Jedi Extracts. As long as there are people like Skywalker and Sloth Bear, there will be makers of erl. For these guys, hash oil is about much more than money. To them, dabs are art, dabs are lifestyle.

The last time I saw Skywalker in person, I was dropping him off at his house after the Secret Cup Finals. He was exhausted from lack of sleep but happy. He had made a new connection with a respected grower who had asked Skywalker to shepherd him through the complexities of the hash-oil market—and to split the profits.

As he gathered his stuff, I told Skywalker I was on my way to Denver because I wanted to see how a government-regulated lab operated with clean CO_2. After all the sneaking around, all the paranoia and janky connections, I was jazzed about witnessing an operation that was legal and safe.

Standing outside the car on the passenger side, James "Skywalker" Johnson leaned into the open window.

"That CO_2 shit tastes like ass breath," he said.

THE POT DOCTOR WILL SEE YOU NOW

A long and jangled day with one of the country's busiest (and most charismatic) cannabis medical professionals.

In a renovated building on the hipster fringes of LA's Skid Row, the pot doctor is open for consultation.

At ten in the morning an alarm is *chime chime chiming* from a laptop in one of two soundproofed cubicles built into the center section of this rectangular thousand-square-foot loft, which also includes a kitchen, a living room area, and the curtained-off bedroom where the pot doctor sleeps. The queue of patients is already full, a virtual line running out the door, into the distressed white marble hallway—a forty-three-year-old mom with panic disorder; a fifty-nine-year-old man with back pain; a thirty-three-year-old clerk with chronic knee pain; a college kid who has trouble getting to sleep at night.

Most of the patients are referrals from an online marijuana delivery service, Eaze, that operates in ninety-some locations around the Golden State. Check the website, order up. Your weed, hash oil, or edibles will be delivered to your door, usually within a half-hour.

But first—at least until pot is legalized in California for recreational use—you need a Medical Marijuana Identification card (MMID).

That's where the pot doc comes in.

* * *

Chime chime chime

Don Davidson flicks a key on his laptop and the face of his first patient appears large on his screen.

"Nice to meet you!" he says into the built-in microphone, upbeat and professional, a little bit amped, moving through his practiced patter at a fair clip.

A graduate of the Virginia Commonwealth University School of Medicine in Richmond, Davidson is thirty-one. He would rather be known by something more dignified than pot doc, something like cannabis doctor, or marijuana MD, but generally, that's what people say: *I need to see the pot doc.* Someday, he hopes, he'll be serving people's medi-card needs in every state in the nation—and selling his complete line of Dr. D. Products.

At the moment, Davidson is the lead physician for EazeMD, a California-based on-demand telemedicine service that pairs licensed physicians with California patients seeking access to medical marijuana. Eaze makes no money from the referral, but approved patients gain immediate access to delivery. By the end of the usual twelve-hour workday, the pot doc and his rotating crew of part-time MDs—working from their own private offices across the state—have recommended cannabis to dozens of patients, who pay the doctors $40 each for their one-year certification, recognized at all dispensaries across the state ($30 for the consultation, $10 for the actual certificate, which is mailed to the patient's home).

As recently as three years ago, a California MMID required a visit to a brick-and-mortar doctor's office. The settings tended to be a bit tawdry; you got the feeling the physicians were on their last hurrah. In some offices, there wasn't even an actual doctor. You sat down at a computer screen in an empty room and waited for one to appear. A medi-card was likely to cost $150 or more. And, of course, you had to go in person.

EazeMD is now in its second year; it is reportedly the largest telemedicine service for pot referrals operating at the moment in California. The queue is busy seven days a week, 10 a.m. until 10 p.m. Sixty patients by 3 p.m. is standard, Davidson says. After 4 p.m., happy hour begins and the number of patients ramps up; it usually stays busy until closing time.

At six foot two and two hundred pounds, the young doctor more than fills his cubicle, which feels a little more expansive thanks to the wall of grimy windows that looks out into the windows of the other lofts around the center courtyard.

A former Division I college tennis player, Davidson is dressed in a skinny Hugo Boss tie and a Hugo Boss dress shirt that shows off a CrossFit-carved physique. His paleo breakfast—hard-boiled egg and avocado—is half-eaten on a paper plate atop the glass desk. Once in a great while, if he's running late, he will forgo the dress pants and Varvatos lace-ups and work in boxer shorts and flip-flops. To his patients he's just a smiling image on a computer screen or smartphone, on a secure version of Skype—a friendly thumbnail with blue eyes and a blondish faux-hawk.

"My name is Dr. Davidson," he says, "and this is a laidback visit, nothing to worry about. Let me run through your chart."

* * *

Don Davidson, MD, is one of a new generation of physicians who see therapeutic value in pot. He is equally an entrepreneur who sees the economic muscle his medical license brings to the biggest growth industry in the nation—valued in 2016, according to an article in *Forbes*, at $7.1 billion, a 26 percent rise over the previous year. Davidson, who declined to reveal his current income, has recently struck a deal with a group of investors that will bring him closer to one of his future goals—a brand of marijuana products of his own.

The son of an orthopedist and a successful catalog model named Kathy Loghry, Davidson grew up on the west side of Richmond, Virginia. While attending James Madison University in Harrisonburg, Virginia—a pre-med student with a modest record of victories as a member of the varsity tennis team—he got his first taste of business success when he helped his older brother start a fresh-baked cookie company on campus. It has since grown into a franchise.

Like many of the munched-out students who were ordering up Campus Cookies, Davidson did, indeed, inhale during his college years and beyond. "I didn't go out and party that much," he says. "I had a 3.9. I studied, worked hard, played sports. And then I smoked some pot on the side. A little cannabis didn't hurt. And it didn't turn me into a leprechaun. It was healthier than drinking, that's for sure."

The summer after his first year of medical school, Davidson started an outfit that led kayaking trips on the Chesapeake Bay. Later, while doing research at the University of Arizona, he opened a web-based date-coaching and lifestyle design service, Dr. D Lifestyle.

"It was just like *Hitch*," he says, referencing the Will Smith movie about a professional date doctor. "We did everything from self-confidence building to fashion help to programs for working out—all men's lifestyle stuff. How to cook better, what to wear, what to say, where to go. I even had one client fly me to Malaysia. It was going really well."

Meanwhile, Davidson says, while studying ventilator-associated pneumonia prevention in the emergency room, he began reading with interest about the sweeping changes that have been remaking the medical and recreational marijuana industries.

"I just saw the writing on the wall, dude," Davidson says with a sly laugh.

"The peer-reviewed papers are fascinating. The science behind this stuff is crazy exciting in a lot of different ways. You've got people using pot instead of taking ibuprofen every day. Or instead of using sleeping pills. Some people are using a high-dose regimen of CBD-rich oils (also called cannabidiol, the pain-relieving ingredient in marijuana) as an adjuvant when battling cancer (as an agent that helps to make their primary treatment work better). Or they're using high CBD oil for seizures. Or they're using it to help suppress Crohn's disease.

"What it comes down to is this: Would you rather have them try a cannabis tincture, three or four drops under their tongue every few hours for pain, appetite, or sleep? Or would you rather give them Celebrex, Wellbutrin, or Xanax—which all have side effects or are addicting?"

* * *

At ten in the evening Davidson closes his laptop; the *chime chime chiming* comes to an end.

While his tie is still perfectly straight, his dress shirt has wilted in the late September heat; his faux-hawk has devolved into a more wind-tossed look. On his desk there is an empty yogurt container, a healthy energy drink, and a few last uneaten chicken nuggets he'd baked for himself in between calls—he hasn't been outside his loft since last night.

All of the consultations with patients are protected by the usual doctor/patient privilege—Davidson can tell me only in general terms who he treated for what. Typically, he spends five to ten minutes with each, discussing general health, specific symptoms, and the advantages of one type of marijuana-based therapy over another. In some cases, Davidson will follow up with links or informational PDFs. Often, he encourages a patient to contact him at a later date with further questions or results.

Over the course of the day, some patients logged in from laptops in dorms, or from desktops in kitchens or offices. Others were on smartphones—one was even driving his car; Davidson insisted he pulled over before continuing. Among the patients, who ranged in age from about nineteen to seventy-eight on this day, a majority complained of migraines, anxiety, pain, inability to sleep. There was a cancer patient; the marijuana helped with her appetite. Complaints of body dysmorphia, lower back pain, and post-traumatic stress were also listed.

In his time in front of the laptop camera, Davidson says, what has struck him most about his patients is their general "distrust of Western medicine, of Big Pharma. They will do anything they can first before they take any sorts of pills. It's not just the people who believe in the healing powers of crystals. These are people who have seen what medicinal drugs can do. They've seen friends get addicted to opiates after a surgery. They've seen people like Prince, like Rush Limbaugh—there's an opioid epidemic ripping through America. If we could have a little cannabis in everyone's cabinet instead of a bunch of pills, I think we would be better off."

When he first dipped into cannabis, Davidson says, he didn't anticipate running an entire operation, or working twelve hours a day. For the last year, since he took over, he's been going seven days a week. The track lights shining down from the high ceiling make deep hollows of his eyes. He hasn't been exercising enough lately. He doesn't get out as much as he should.

But he knows a bonanza when he sees it. He's willing to put in the time.

"After doing a surgical residency, I know how to sleep on the floor, eat shit, and get yelled at," he muses. "At least now I'm working for myself."

Drifting away from his cubicle, Davidson heads toward the living room side of the space, two big sofas and a TV. His part-time admin staff—a USC-trained registered nurse with experience running dispensaries, and an IT guy who sometimes sleeps on the couch after a long day—have left for the evening.

The loft is quiet and still. The sounds of weeknight domesticity swirl around the courtyard and drift in through the open windows—music and laughter, the clatter of plates, the yapping of a small dog. On one shelf is a display of pot paraphernalia used for instructional video posts—a large vaporizer, a bong, an assortment of vape pens for hash oil. On another is a collection of health supplements—vitamins and protein powders and energy boosts.

Everywhere around the room are partially packed boxes. Things have been going well. The lease on the loft expires soon. He's planning to move his operation to a house in Malibu with a view of the ocean. Like he said: If he's going to spend all day, every day in a cubicle seeing patients via the Internet, "it might as well be one at the beach with a big window."

Davidson lowers himself onto the sofa and uncoils, loosens his tie. He looks at his watch and sighs.

In barely twelve hours, it will begin again.

Chime. Chime. Chime.

He reaches for the bong.

MEETING THE GHOST OF CHRISTMAS FUTURE

After a questionable police raid on his house in Woody Creek, Colorado, the legendary journalist and *Rolling Stone* National Affairs Chief Hunter S. Thompson is charged with possession of illegal drugs and faces a fifty-year prison sentence. Going on high alert, the home office immediately dispatches a young Mike Sager to the scene. The next three weeks will teach at least one of them lessons to last a lifetime.

THE TRIAL OF HUNTER S. THOMPSON

Owl Farm sits peacefully above Woody Creek Road, hunkered behind a locked gate, guarded by a pair of tin vultures perched on ten-foot poles. A log cabin, an outbuilding, a satellite dish, a bullet-riddled BMW, a couple of barking peacocks—110 acres in all, nestled against a hillside in the springtime bloom of Roaring Fork Valley.

Five miles northwest of glitzy Aspen, Colorado, this is the home of Dr. Hunter S. Thompson, progenitor of gonzo journalism, chief of ROLLING STONE'S National Affairs Desk, self-described "lazy drunken hillbilly with a heart full of hate who has found a way to live out there where the real winds blow—to sleep late, have fun, get wild, drink whiskey and drive fast on empty streets with nothing in mind except falling in love and not getting arrested." For the past twenty-four years, Thompson has lived here in jangled seclusion, doing his damnedest to follow his motto, "Let the good times roll."

These days, however, the times are not so good. After an eleven-hour search of his home by six law-enforcement officers, Thompson has been charged with five felonies and three misdemeanors. The warrant for the search, based upon the reluctant cooperation of an LA porno producer turned Michigan ophthalmologist's wife, was executed on February 26, and the search continued into the early morning hours of the 27th. Among the items seized were the following: .09 gram (about one line) of cocaine, three Valium-like tablets, thirty-nine hits of LSD, a hookah purchased in the Haight in the sixties, a BIC pen shell with white-powder residue, an antique Gatling gun, seven ounces of marijuana, and four sticks of dynamite, found in the Xerox room. Largely due to the drug- and dynamite-possession charges, Thompson faces up to fifty years in prison.

"The whole thing's driving me crazy," says Thompson, throwing another slice of sausage into an iron skillet. It's dinner time on the farm, and Thompson is cooking up a feast: salmon croquettes, peas and corn, spring onions, tomatoes, pimentos, pumpernickel, grapes, grapefruit, and anything arranged on a large cutting board for a buffet. The NBA playoffs are on the wide screen; two private detectives, hired by Thompson's attorney, are in the other room, drawing diagrams, poking through drawers. Research materials for Thompson's next book, *Songs of the Doomed*, are scattered everywhere, and a memo to the home office in New York City is humming into the fax machine, screaming headline suggestions for this story: POLICE RUN AMOK IN ASPEN'S GILDED CAGE—FORMER SHERIFF CANDIDATE PUT ON TRIAL BY SLEAZY CABAL OF DRUNKARDS, CRIMINALS & JESUS FREAKS: ONE-TIME VALHALLA TAKEN OVER BY NAZIS & GREEDHEADS.

A couple of friends are over, drinking beer, doing errands, washing dishes, lending support, talking about selling T-shirts for the Hunter S. Thompson Legal Defense Fund. Thompson's assistant is due back tomorrow. The book is due May 21. The preliminary hearing is scheduled for May 22.

Thompson careens through the kitchen/writing area in white Converse sneakers, his reading glasses down low on his nose, a butcher knife in his hand, blood trickling from his finger. He is fifty-two now, graying, with just the hint of a potbelly, remarkably fit for a man whose doctor greets him at his physical each year with an incredulous "You're still alive?" In fact, the lines are deep in his face, and the wear of all those years running at the red line is beginning to show. But he is remarkably spry, still the man he once described as "a doctor of chemotherapy . . . with the physical constitution of a mule shark and a brain as rare and sharp and original as the Sloat diamond." If only there wasn't this case.

"Like right now," Thompson is saying, gesturing with the knife, wiping the blood, "I have seven things to do, and I can't do them. I'm focusing all my energy on the case, when I should be focusing on the book. There's nobody on the book's team. The book is outnumbered. It gets overwhelmed. I haven't done nearly enough editing. The writing is a place to hide.

"I have no time to myself," he says, fitting another Dunhill into his signature cigarette holder. "I don't have time to read a newspaper. I feel pushed. Angry. I don't have any time even to be with a woman. The worst thing is that I've been taken out of what I do best. I have to think like a lawyer, a secretary. The phone is ringing. The Xerox is broken. I have to be security conscious. I can't trust people. I can't think. I can't do my writing.

"This whole thing seems to me like a joke. Worse things happen in a lot of people's houses. When I was told about the complaint, I couldn't remember it. I thought it was a woman up the road who was bitching about me shooting. I hadn't been shooting, as it happens, but I thought it was the usual type of thing. I didn't ask to be here. Maybe I did, in a way. Maybe the times have changed around me. There's no doubt about it. This was a lifestyle twist."

* * *

It had all started innocently enough. Sometime in January, Thompson had received a handwritten note on a turquoise card from a fan named Gail Palmer-Slater. Tall and thick-lipped, the thirty-five-year-old Palmer-Slater had been a director and producer of porno films. She'd begun her career at nineteen, when she landed a gig at an X-rated theater in Michigan, impersonating a famous porn star, signing autographs. The next year, the Michigan State coed became one of Playboy magazine's "Girls of the Big Ten." After that, Palmer-Slater moved to California, and in 1975 she produced her first film, *Hot Summer in the City*. She went on to make eight more, including *Hot Legs*, *Fantasy World*, *California Gigolo*, and *The Erotic Adventures of Candy*.

Recently, however, Palmer-Slater appeared to be leading the straight life. She'd been married to an eye doctor for the past two years and was living in rural St. Clair, Michigan. The couple was scheduled to attend an ophthalmologists' convention in Snowmass, a resort community near Aspen. A big fan of Thompson's, she'd read every one of his books. She herself was trying to be a writer and had stacks of her own unproduced screenplays on a shelf at home, along with several chapters of an autobiography, she wanted to do a project with Thompson, maybe use her old Hollywood connections to make a movie of *Fear and Loathing in Las Vegas*. She didn't know if Thompson would agree to see her, but what the heck, it was worth a try.

"I said on the card to Hunter that I'd read in *Generation of Swine* his references to the adult industry and that I used to work in that industry," Palmer-Slater said in a telephone interview with *Rolling Stone*. "I said I thought there were some things he might enjoy talking about."

On February 21, Palmer-Slater said, she got a call at her Snowmass hotel, the Wildwood Inn, from a man named Semmes. The man pointed out that his name was the same spelled backward or forward. He invited Palmer-Slater up to Owl Farm. Take a taxi, he told her, all the drivers know where it is.

Palmer-Slater got to Thompson's around 6:30 p.m. What happened next is in dispute. Thompson, noting the pending case, will not discuss the incidents of that night. In a taped interview with an investigator from the DA's office, Palmer-Slater said that after she arrived, she sat around with Thompson, his female writing assistant, and two of his male friends, talking, watching the Grammys, drinking margaritas and vodka and cranberry juice. At some point, Palmer-Slater said, she asked Thompson about his sexual preferences, and he had her read aloud from an unpublished piece of his called "Screwjack," an account of a sexual escapade between Thompson and his black tomcat.

As the night wore on, according to a transcript of Palmer-Slater's interview with the investigator, a dish of white powder was passed around the room. Then Thompson allegedly asked Palmer-Slater to join him in his hot tub. Palmer-Slater claims that when she refused, Thompson became an angry and called her a "lesbian bitch." According to Palmer-Slater, he then twisted her left breast with his right hand, pushed her, threw a drink at her and yelled at her to get out. Palmer-Slater said she went outside, where she was consoled by Thompson's assistant until a cab came to take her back to her hotel.

When she returned to her hotel, according to the transcript, Palmer-Slater and her husband, Dr. Charles Slater, discussed the incident, then called Marco DiMercurio, Palmer's former boyfriend and porn-business partner, in Los Angeles. Next, the police say, Dr. Slater telephoned the Aspen police dispatcher and reported the incident. Sometime later, according to the police, DiMercurio called the Aspen police and claimed that Thompson had held a gun to Palmer-Slater's head. The exact time of Dr. Slater's call is not known. According to the police, there is no record of the call. Routinely, each call to the dispatcher is tape-recorded. But when the tapes were reviewed, no such call was found. In addition, the little card that is customarily filled out upon receipt of a complaint was missing.

Upon hearing of the complaint, Pitkin County sheriff Bob Braudis, a longtime friend of Thompson's who is up for reelection this year, withdrew from the case, transferring it to the DA's office.

* * *

In the last twenty-five years, as Aspen has grown and prospered, and property values have soared, the nonconformists and athletic flower children who set the tone for happy, freewheeling Aspen in the sixties have been replaced by millionaires in the seventies and then billionaires in the eighties. Today, Aspen is a study in quaint.

It is well-scrubbed and fussy, with ordinances against neon and smoking, a ski and shopping town that has been called "a salt lick for celebrities" and "a petting zoo for the rich and famous." Every year during the ski season, the stars and moguls arrive in droves. More than half the landings at Aspen's tiny airport are made by private planes, and Range Rovers are so commonplace that a special service representative flies in from Denver once or twice a week during the season to do warranty work. This year, the average home in Aspen costs over $1.4 million. Historic buildings have been torn down and replaced by condos; affordable housing is in such short supply that operations like the Little Nell hotel—with suites going for up to $2,000 a night in season—are busing their help from as far as seventy miles down valley. The last director of the town's art museum quit, in part, because she couldn't find a two-bedroom apartment for less than $2,000 a month.

In this new Aspen era of money and studied glamour, Milton Blakey, the local district attorney, based down valley in conservative Glenwood Springs, has decided to wage his own local War on Drugs. In a town where at one time, according to longtime resident Michael Solheim, "you could go into a bar and everyone in the room would have a little blow in their pocket," Blakey's office has recently prosecuted cases as small as the alleged sale of twenty-five dollars' worth of cocaine. Blakey is reported to be seeking a judgeship.

Many familiar with Thompson's case say that the bust smacked of personal vendetta. Others say it is simply a sign of the political climate in America today, another example of law enforcement and the courts chipping away at Fourth Amendment rights in the name of the national drug crusade.

"With the influx of all the new money, Thompson doesn't fit into what they want in this resort," says David Matthews-Price, the editor of Aspen's *Daily Times*.

Through the years, Thompson has lived in relative peace in Woody Creek. There has been the odd feud with a rich neighbor, and the odd Thompsonesque prank, like the time he threw smoke bombs into Woody Creek Tavern, his favorite haunt, just down the road from Owl Farm. But the fact is, Thompson has published six best-selling books and countless magazine and newspaper articles, most of which document his frenzied intake of alcohol, nicotine, and illegal drugs. And in all those years—except for the time he was fined for pulling a shotgun out of his golf bag on a local course and blasting an airborne golf ball to smithereens—no one has much bothered him. In 1970, he even ran for the office of sheriff, campaigning on a "Freak Power" platform, one of whose planks was to rename Aspen "Fat City"—in order to discourage "greedheads and land rapers" from overrunning the town. Thompson lost by 465 votes. Today he enjoys pointing out that all his predictions came true.

Following the phone calls from Slater and DiMercurio on the night of February 21, DA investigator Michael Kelly visited Palmer-Slater at her hotel the next afternoon. At that point, Palmer-Slater gave the tape-recorded interview that spelled out her version of what had happened in the house: the drinks, the Grammys, the drugs, the hot tub, the altercation. She also told Kelly that, contrary to what DiMercurio had said, no gun had been pointed at her and that she didn't think Thompson's hot-tub invitation had any real sexual motive.

Kelly listened for about an hour and then, according to the transcript, told Palmer-Slater: "I can tell you that it appears to me like you were assaulted .... Oftentimes we defer to the wishes of the victim, your [sic] the one that was victimized here. The mere fact that you don't want to prosecute doesn't necessarily mean we won't."

In her *Rolling Stone* interview, Palmer-Slater said that she had told Kelly she was not interested in prosecuting Thompson. "I really laid it out, kind of pleaded my case," she said, "I told him that because I was the first female producer of X-rated movies, because I started out as a Michigan State student, every news bureau in the United States has clippings about me. When you give my name, don't think that I'm just some unknown. But [Kelly] said, 'Gail, he may do something again that will be worse.' He said they'd get back to me. He said, 'We don't need your permission to go ahead and prosecute.' Which I didn't even know. If I had, I might not have even told the whole episode. I got caught in the middle. I feel like the police are using me."

Without interviewing any of the others present at Owl Farm that night, Blakey's lieutenant, chief deputy DA Chip McCrory, drew up misdemeanor charges for assault and sexual assault, and asked an Aspen judge for a warrant to search Thompson's home. The local judge passed on signing, whereupon McCrory took it to a more accommodating judge in Glenwood Springs, sixty miles away.

Three days later, McCrory and Kelly met with Sheriff Broadis. According to press accounts of the meeting, when it was suggested that a single-source search warrant might not stand up in court, McCrory pounded his fist on the table. "If we go out and interview other people who were there, we're going to blow this warrant out of the water," McCrory reportedly said. McCrory also insisted that because Thompson was armed and violent, the sheriff should put together a SWAT team to arrest him. The sheriff, however, thought that a telephone call to Thompson would suffice. Reached at home, Thompson promptly came down to the sheriff's office, where he was booked on the assault and sexual-assault charges. That afternoon, the search warrant was executed by Kelly and five sheriff's deputies. Following lab tests of the take, five felony charges were filed against Thompson on April 9. He was freed on a $2,000 bond. (At the preliminary hearing on May 22, as we went to press, one felony charge involving cocaine use was dropped. In addition, Palmer-Slater testified that she'd been urged to contact Thompson by a "freelance undercover agent" who has worked for federal and state law-enforcement officials. She did not elaborate. Another hearing is set for June 25.)

* * *

"They've been after me for a long time," says Thompson, at home in his kitchen, popping a beer-soaked piece of sausage into his mouth. "People think I should be rehabilitated. The message I'm getting is that the times are a-changin'. In a way, maybe the times changed around me. There are no rebels anymore. I really don't fit in here anymore. It's sort of like being the last cowboy."

Thompson's attorney, Harold Haddon, says he believes "the basic issue in this case is whether a writer's privacy can be invaded in an eleven-hour search that covers every nook and cranny of his house, sniffs into his papers, his videos, everything. It's a real test of whether the Fourth Amendment has any meaning."

Thompson agrees. "The legal system has changed," he says. "The Nixon-Reagan-Bush Supreme Court has almost destroyed the Fourth Amendment, the guarantee against unreasonable search and seizure. The burden of proof has shifted to the accused. It used to be on the accuser, the police. In my case what they did was get some dingbat who came into my house. The complaint was insane.

"All they did was use her in this. She thought she saw me using drugs. That was enough for them to come search my house. And Christ, they found what—nine one-hundredths of one gram? It wouldn't be worth licking off a bindle. They claim they found some acid. I'm charged with felony possession of Valium. It's what you'd call a really ugly fishing expedition. Felony possession of dynamite, which was left there by the ditch-digging company. These low-rent, bush-league, white-trash cops, these pigs, they decided to use whatever they could just to come after me. Because, hey, I'm too dangerous. I'm too weird to be wandering around. That's their thinking.

"I think basically that the War on Drugs has become the bogeyman that will replace the cold war. The army's trying will replace the cold war. The army's trying to get into the war now, too. They have nothing else to do.

"ABC News ran a poll recently that really scared the hell out of me. It shows that something like 52 percent of the people polled are in favor of random searches of people's houses for drugs. And something like 83 percent were in favor of turning in anybody involved with drugs, even if they happen to be a member of your own family.

"This is really like Germany in 1933. People are not going to like it too much when their neighbor gets pissed off at the music being too loud and calls the cops and says, 'I think Joe over there is doing drugs. I saw him picking his nose in front of the window with a cigarette. He acts like a dope fiend. You better investigate.'

"I'm not guilty at all. They're guilty. The bastards attacked my house. They want me to cop a plea to dynamite or some crazy shit. I told them, "There are two things I would plead guilty to: One is having a twenty-year-old brass hookah that I got on Haight Street. The other is, I'd be willing to go to dynamite rehab in order to learn more about explosives.' No, I probably can't do that. Dynamite is one of the felonies, isn't it? They want me on probation. They want me within the system. Within the system is a new buzzword in law enforcement. They can keep an eye on me there. I'll have to start obeying rules that aren't even rules.

"The thing is, they've confused the artist with the art. To a large extent, if I'd done half of what I wrote, I'd be dead."

—Rolling Stone, June 26, 1990

CHARGES DROPPED AGAINST HUNTER THOMPSON

"I beat the goddam swine," crowed Dr. Hunter S. Thompson, following a state district judge's dismissal of four remaining felony and three misdemeanor charges against him.

The charges of assault, sexual assault, and illegal possession of drugs and explosives stemmed from an alleged alteration between Thompson and a former porno producer who visited the chief of ROLLING STONE'S National Affairs Desk at his Woody Creek, Colorado, farm, near Aspen, in February. Following a preliminary hearing on May 22, the case was dismissed by state district court judge Charles Buss at the request of prosecutors, who said that they would be "unable to establish guilt beyond a reasonable doubt."

The decision to drop the case "was made after an evaluation of the preliminary-hearing testimony," said Pitkin County DA Milt Blakey following the judge's ruling. The investigation, according to the DA, was hampered by the refusal of several key witness, friends of Thompson's who were at his house during the incident, to speak with investigators.

The DA also cited "discrepancies between sworn testimony and previous statements to investigators," resulting in "the conclusion that the people would be unable to sustain their burden of proof."

Thompson, the progenitor of gonzo journalism, has written six best-selling books and countless newspaper and magazine articles documenting his frenzied intake of alcohol, nicotine, and illegal drugs over the last quarter of a century. He has asserted that his run-in with authorities amounted to a "lifestyle bust," one that was precipitated by changing attitudes in glitzy Aspen and by the nation's recent war on drugs, which, he believes, "has become the bogeyman that will replace the cold war."

Thompson's problems with the law began on February 21, when he was visited by a fan named Gail Palmer-Slater, a thirty-five-year-old former Playboy "Girl of the Big Ten" who went on to produce or direct nine hard-core porn movies. Palmer-Slater, who retired a number of years ago from the adult industry and married an ophthalmologist, has been leading the straight life in rural St. Clair, Michigan. She wrote Thompson in January, saying that she and her husband would be attending an ophthalmologists' convention at a ski resort nearby and requesting a meeting with the author.

Upon arrival at Owl Farm, Thompson's home, Palmer-Slater told investigators, she joined Thompson, his female assistant, and two of his friends as they watched the Grammys and had a few drinks. During her visit, Palmer-Slater alleged, a dish of white powder was passed around the room. At some point after Palmer-Slater asked Thompson a question about his sexual preferences, she said the journalist showed her his hot tub. When she refused to join him in the tub, she said, Thompson became angry, called her a "lesbian bitch," twisted her left breast with his right hand, pushed her, threw a drink at her, and yelled at her to get out.

Thompson, however, claimed that Palmer-Slater had made the sexual advances toward him, and that she was "sloppy drunk." He denied asking her into the hot tub, explaining that "she would have displaced too much water."

Against Palmer-Slater's wishes and without interviewing any other witnesses, the DA's office asked an Aspen judge for a warrant to search Thompson's home. The local judge reportedly declined to order the search, whereupon the DA's office took the request to a more accommodating judge over sixty miles away.

Thompson's log cabin was then searched for eleven hours by six law-enforcement officers. Among the items seized were .09 gram (about one line) of cocaine, three Valium-like tablets, thirty-nine hits of LSD, a BIC-pen shell with white-powder residue, seven ounces of marijuana, and four sticks of dynamite. Largely due to the drug and dynamite-possession charges, Thompson faced up to fifty years in prison.

Problems with the prosecution's case surfaced immediately. It was reported that chief deputy DA Chip McCrory, at a meeting of law-enforcement officials, pounded his fist on the table and said, "If we go out and interview other people who were there, we're going to blow this warrant out of the water."

At the preliminary hearing in state district court in Aspen on May 22, the prosecution's case broke down further. Under questioning, Palmer-Slater contradicted her earlier statements to investigators, saying that she couldn't be sure that the white powder she saw in Thompson's house was actually cocaine. On cross-examination by Thompson's attorney, Hal Haddon, Palmer-Slater also admitted that while she saw Thompson holding a BIC pen shell and a dish of white powder, she couldn't recall seeing him inhale the substance.

The hearing proceeded in gonzo fashion before a packed gallery, with Thompson muttering, groaning, smacking his forehead with his palm, passing notes to spectators and, according to Palmer-Slater, even fluttering his eyelashes Groucho-style at her.

Outside, more than one hundred people gathered for the off-season show—a group that included fans, journalists, and such members of the adult industry as the Mitchell Brothers, a pair of porn producers who had led a caravan from San Francisco to show solidarity with Thompson.

At the first hearing, Judge Buss dropped a felony cocaine-use charge against Thompson. A week later, DA Blakey decided not to pursue the case further, saying, "We should've looked more closely early on for evidence that would've established conclusively his possession of the contraband. We didn't get that." Blakey also cited problems linking Thompson to the drugs found in his house. The defense was prepared to argue that friends or relatives had left the drugs and dynamite at Thompson's place.

When questioned about her role in the Thompson case by *Rolling Stone*, Palmer-Slater said, "I'm glad it's over. I think my testimony was weaker than they would have liked it. I'm glad Hunter won. If they were out to help a victim, why didn't they just go after the assault charge? I'm thinking that they were out for Hunter. I asked them, 'How come you're not just doing the assault?' and they said, 'It doesn't carry enough jail time.' It's a shame—an assault is a misdemeanor but someone doing drugs in their own house can be a felony."

Michael Solheim, a longtime Thompson friend and advisor, said reaction in the Thompson camp was "enormous jubilation and surprise. We knew that these guys were embarrassed, we knew they had a lousy case. When it was over, the feeling was 'Jesus! Goddamn it! What are we going to do this summer now?'"

Solheim also implied that the Thompson affair may not be over. "We are looking carefully at the possibility of going into a civil action against the government for harassing Hunter," he said.

According to Solheim and Haddon, evidence surfaced during preparation for the trial that federal agents may have had Thompson under surveillance for as long as two months before the Palmer-Slater incident. In addition, an investigator in the case has been accused of surreptitiously taping a privileged conversation between Thompson and one of his attorneys that took place at the DA's office.

Thompson's defense will end up costing over $100,000, says Solheim, who added that any remaining monies from the Hunter S. Thompson Legal Defense Fund would be made available to others "who find themselves in similar situations throughout the country."

"They fled like rats into the darkness," Thompson said of the prosecution, prior to a lengthy "celebration orgy" at Woody Creek Tavern. "Everybody's house is a lot safer today. If we'd lost this case, they'd have been at your house next."

—*Rolling Stone*, July 12–28, 1990

THE MORNING COKE: ON BEING HUNTER S. THOMPSON'S ASSISTANT FOR THREE WEEKS

Elian Peltier: HST was arrested in late February 1990. What did he represent for journalism at that time?
Mike Sager: Hunter did come from the age when writers could be celebrities. The writers and journalists were the movie stars and TV producers of earlier eras. And Hunter was the gold standard, a cult figure but well known.

His writing and what he sort of stood for was descended from the tradition of the Beat writers of the 1950s and 1960s, and even before: going back to William Burroughs, Henry Miller, and Paul Bowles, this chain of writers who labored in the fields of experimentation, drugs, and decadence.

Hunter Thompson comes out of that tradition, but he started as a newspaper writer, as did many of the other great New Journalists, including at the top of the list Tom Wolfe and Gay Talese. They were the progenitors of the Golden Age of magazine writing.

At the same time, Hunter was doing something different than Wolfe and Talese. Though all were highly stylized in one manner or another, Wolfe and Talese stuck more to the actual facts. They deployed their reportage in a literary style, thought with a strict adherence to newspaper standards of fact-checking. Hunter would use his press card as a sort of ticket to embellish. He lived in this giant glass fishbowl that was full of smoke, so that the reality he saw was sort of filtered. He liked to interpret truth and sort of bend (or break it) in the interest of his own dramatic ends. Though he was always the type of reporter who would embed himself within the subject he was reporting, early in his career, in classic works like *Hell's Angels* and *The Great Shark Hunt*, he was more straight-laced. His work was energetic and entertaining. Not always 100 percent true, however. Very impressionistic. He saw life as a wild ride. His pieces had great pace and energy because of that.

EP: How would you describe his style, beyond "gonzo journalism"?
MS: What Hunter Thompson was doing was taking the tenets of literary journalism—taking the facts and applying literary principles to them, such as scenes, settings, characters, dialogues, descriptions—one step further. He made it into a first-person drama.

To me, he was like a meat grinder: he takes all the shit in, churns it through himself, and the product he spewed out was a picture of a reality only he could see.

EP: Let's come back to his trial, in 1990, and the piece you were assigned to write about him for *Rolling Stone*. What was it like?
MS: When Hunter got arrested in late February of 1990 and was charged with five felonies and three misdemeanors, everybody got super grandiose. Hunter was always grandiose; when you entered his life and his world, you became the same. When he sent me out to cover Hunter and his story, the owner of *Rolling Stone*, Jann Wenner, sent him a fax (which was the way Hunter liked to communicate), *"We're sending you Mike Sager, he's one of our best!"* I immediately felt as if I was on a mission. This was no mere story. This was a journey to the Heart of Hunter.

The search took place in late February of 1990; I went there in early March. All I needed was an interview with him, and *Rolling Stone* gave me two weeks.

But let's add two things, very frankly: first, I was a biased reporter from the home office who was being sent out partially because the editor was helping Hunter, and partially because we had an inside track to Hunter, who always made a great story. And, of course, his arrest was making headlines. And *Rolling Stone* loved to Question Authority, as they used to say in the 1960s and 1970s. *Rolling Stone* was the *New York Times* of the counterculture. Hunter was the poster boy.

So I was a member of the press, but I was a biased member of the press, a colleague, and also a huge fan. I felt like I was there more to help out. It turned out I stayed three weeks. In the end it kind of felt like I was visiting the Ghost of Christmas Future.

EP: What was a typical day like?
MS: Everything was jangled, with electricity in the air, a sense of movement, and discomfort, and excitement.

I remember that when I would get to his place in the late mornings, all of his peacocks would be perched high in the trees. They have this eerie bark; they sound like dogs from hell. The sky was gray and cloudy and foreboding.

After I was there a few days we settled into a routine. I'd come over to the house as he was waking up.

The first thing he would do is hand me a baggie containing about a quarter ounce of cocaine.

Back in these days, coke was purer. It was rocky, and crystalline. He had a piece of paraphernalia that was common to the day, it was called a Deering Blender, it looked kind of like the type of grinders you see used today for marijuana, with teeth inside. All their products were Tiffany blue. The blender had a crank on the top. It would turn the rocks into powder, suitable for snorting.

I would dump the entire quarter ounce into the grinder, and grind it over a mirror. When I was finished there would be a little snowdrift of coke on the mirror, like a little mountain. Hunter would take one of those old BIC Pens—a tube of clear-plastic—and he'd remove the ink cartridge. It made a perfect straw. It even had a little hole in the side you could use as a "carburetor." He'd bend over, stick the pen into the snowdrift, and do a huge snort. And the day would begin. You never knew what cosmic plain you'd end up on by day's end.

EP: So every day would start with the morning coke?
MS: Drugs were a ritual. Like everything, it was very grandiose. I played the role of the butler. He would hand me the baggie with great ceremony, like I had a precious job on my hands—a quarter ounce in those days was worth over $500 bucks, so I guess it was pretty precious. What you learned was that everything in Hunter's world was, like they say on Broadway, *louder, faster, funnier*. It was like we were in this madcap comedy-drama.

Then the day would continue from there and last about thirty-six hours—we'd be coking and smoking and drinking and rolling joints the whole time. In the meantime, we'd be getting a semblance of work done.

At that time, he was writing a column for the *San Francisco Examiner*. Because all I needed from him for my story were some quotes, and because he had no assistant—she had quit after the arrest, fearful of becoming involved—I volunteered to become his new, temporary assistant.

He would work in the kitchen, on a highchair at the sink, over which he'd placed a wooden board on which he set his typewriter, which he was still using in the early days of desktop computing. Across from him, mounted on the wall, was a huge TV screen hooked to a satellite feed, both of which were uncommon in that era.

He would get up, make breakfast, start eating something and answering faxes at the same time, and random people would start coming over to his house. All day long he'd be typing, faxing, making grandiose phone calls, meanwhile attending to other tasks that drew his attention—like he would take a box of salmon croquettes out of the freezer, open a beer, make himself a margarita, start sharpening all of his knives, cut himself, bleed all over the place. He ordered me to start fires in his huge stone fireplace with gasoline and I would do so—at one point I was starting the fire and it kind of exploded and I gashed my bald head on a huge rusty nail and it bled like hell. I felt like I was becoming part of the jangled drama that was his everyday life.

My duties: I would make copies, search for files among his scattered papers, fetch more beer or tequila, roll joints, call out for pizza. We'd have adventures, like we'd go shoot something in the yard. He loved guns (he would later take his own life with a firearm), so we'd go out and take target practice. There were old cars scattered in his back acreage and we'd shoot at them. Or he would decide some books had to be shot, which he would then autograph and sell as art.

Some days, we'd go down to the Woody Creek Tavern for lunch. It was cold but he insisted on driving his convertible with the top down. He'd order everything on the menu, and we would have a million drinks and people would join us.

By night, when it was time for me to leave, he'd give me a pile of notes and half-written ideas and a gram of coke and send me back to my room at the Little Nell Hotel to reassemble/retype/edit his columns. The next day, we'd submit by fax to his editor. I think we got three done over the time I was there. I can't remember for the life of me what they were about.

Every thirty-six-hour session ended differently. One night he'd shoot his gun up into the ceiling of his living room to make his assembled visitors clear out. The next night he'd calmly ask if I could leave early because a woman was coming to visit.

"Sometimes you just need a hug," he told me, showing me his soft underbelly. From that moment on, I loved him. I saw him as a whole different figure. Still great, but exceptionally lonely.

I remember, one night he was sending this huge fax to his mother. Page after page. And he's using these different colors, like pens, only the fax only transmits black and white. At some point his elderly mother became annoyed and sent a fax of her own. "Stop sending me faxes, you're using all my paper."

EP: Did he have a lot of friends in Aspen?
MS: He was definitely the exuberant guy. He would enter the room and bring a whole world in with him. Friends would always be stopping by the house. He was just a party on the roll. Everywhere he went, he was Bacchus, the god of partying. Let the good times roll. That was one of his many slogans.

EP: How do you remember this time with him, more than twenty-five years later?
MS: The time I spent with Hunter was totally surreal. I was swept into this grandiose thing. It's life+ when you're with him.

Good journalism has that louder, faster, funnier quality that Hunter brought to the work. It is, after all, entertainment. Or INFOtainment, though at its highest form. Hunter was paid to be the party boy, to be louder, faster, funnier, drunker, more fucked up. Everybody wanted to be like him. That's why he has such a strong, cult following, which remains strong after his death.

He was smart, he was fun to be around, but he was also so sweet. He would allow himself to go beyond where most responsible people go. And he got paid for it. His life became his work and his work was his. Everything was a story.

This is why, during that period, I allowed myself to experience that same sort of life. You get sleep-deprived on a thirty-six-hour schedule, you're kind of jet-lagged, everything is melting between spring and winter, cemented, frozen in time. The peacocks are screaming, the sky is gray, Hunter is on a roll, moving here to there around the room, doing all his projects, real and imagined. All while doing a ton of drugs.

I started to feel the way Hunter S. Thompson must have felt. Everything became a sort of a blur. And thus he perceived everything from within the smoke-filled fishbowl of his own mad genius.

One thing I learned from Hunter S. Thompson is that I don't work on hard drugs. I'm definitely not Hunter S. Thompson. I'm not flinging myself over the cliff. I'm a cautious person even though I crave knowledge and experience. I'd rather crawl up to the ledge, look over, see what's going on. I don't have a death wish. Just a wish to learn the world and to make art from it.

EP: How was *Rolling Stone* at that time?
MS: We are in 1990. Hunter is fifty-two, I am thirty-four. I had my first story for them in 1984 and I started to work there under contract around '87.

The offices were in New York, 745 5th Avenue, on one corner of Central Park. All the walls had the legendary rock and roll photos by famous photographers like Annie Liebovitz; I always remember seeing the famous shot of John Lennon and Yoko Ono in bed, with John naked, wrapped around the clothed Yoko.

The first time I visited the RS offices, around 1983, the editor was David Rosenthal. On his window was a bottle of Jack Daniel's and some sort of a bird, a parrot I think? That was my first contact with *Rolling Stone*.

EP: Did you ever have contact with him after your sojourn with him?
MS: Not long after my story in *Rolling Stone*, *Esquire* hired Hunter to do some stories. They wanted to resurrect his brand.

On one occasion *Esquire* brought Hunter to New York, I happened to be there also, working on my story about the Pope of Pot. As we read in the title story of this collection, the pope had a marijuana delivery service, the first of its kind.

At the time *RS* used to put me up in the Hotel Chelsea, another legendary countercultural place; not surprisingly, a good number of the longtime residents (it had long-term guests and short) knew the pope.

I had a regular room, nothing to speak of, dreary corridors, mismatched furniture, a threadbare bedspread, a desultory telephone operator on the first floor presiding over the old-fashioned switchboard—you would stop by the front desk on your way in to get your messages, scribbled on the kind of standard note paper sold in those days for that purpose. Of course, besides the ornate iron grillwork, classic awning, and iconic neon sign adorning the front of the red brick building, there was nothing more impressive than the lobby, with its array of outstanding art traded over the years to the owner by various starving artists in exchange for rent. Of course, the array of people were the biggest draw: often I would sit in the lobby and watch the passing show. Any time of day or night, a ride in one of the slow, ancient, push-button elevators—paneled with rich red-brown wood—was an adventure. One night at a room party given by a semi-permanent resident (there were long-timers as well as night-to-night guests), I met Huncke the Junkie. He was old as fuck, attended by youngish men who were said to do all his heroin scoring for him, now that he was in his dotage. I kind of got the sense that he'd been pickled by decades of use.

Anyway, Hunter was being stewarded (and enabled) around New York by *Esquire* editor David Hirshey, for whom I'd also done some work, and who would later become a great friend. One morning at about four a.m., I woke up to a frantic call from Hirshey. There was a crisis. Hunter Thompson has lost his ball of hash. He needed replacement weed. And fast.

I hung up the phone and called the Pope of Pot. Within an hour, one of the pope's bicycle messengers was making a delivery at Hunter's hotel.

Definitely among the top five moments of my life. How fucking cool was I?

I'm pretty sure Hunter never forgot either. A few few years later, he'd give me a blurb for my first book. From what I've been able to gather, it's the only blurb he ever gave.

Of course, I had to call him literally 50 times before his then-assistant (and future widow), Anita, took pity on me and expedited the process by reading Hunter the entire first chapter of *Scary Monsters and Super Freaks*. I will always be thankful to both of them. Of course, the news of Hunter's death was both shocking and horrible.

And totally in character.

EP: You told me earlier, "I'm definitely not Hunter S. Thompson! I'm not going to stand on the edge of the cliff, I want to live." Hunter took his own life at home in 2005. Why would you say Thompson wasn't willing to live longer?
MS: Well, that's a hard one. Who knows? I can't say. I do know that he shot and killed himself with his son and his grandson in a different part of the house. That's the action of a person who wasn't exactly right in the mind.

The only hint I've been able to offer myself has been this tidbit of knowledge:

Right before he died, there was a party for Hunter in New Orleans, where his literary editor lives. By that time he was confined to a wheelchair due to various unspecified health problems. When his party arrived at the bar, it turned out the festivities were being held in a private room *up a steep set of stairs.*

I don't know if nobody was strong enough to bodily carry Hunter's wheelchair (or Hunter) up the stairs. I don't know if anyone suggested it. Or tried. But I do know Hunter did not attend his own fucking party. Can you imagine how he felt? He was supposed to be the most Gonzo of them all. The partier's partier. His career had gotten started with a macho (and dangerous) stint embedded with the Hell's Angels. He shot guns, did more drugs than anyone, and lived to tell about it in a lively and entertaining style.

As he once, and very famously wrote: "Maybe there is no Heaven. Or maybe this is all pure gibberish—a product of the demented imagination of a lazy drunken hillbilly with a heart full of hate who has found a way to live out where the real winds blow—to sleep late, have fun, get wild, drink whisky, and drive fast on empty streets with nothing in mind except falling in love and not getting arrested . . . Res ipsa loquitur. Let the good times roll."

Soon after he came back home to Woody Creek, he killed himself.

—Interview of Mike Sager by Elian Peltier for Ulyces.co, March 24, 2016

Interview conducted in English.
Translated from the French.
Edited for clarity: August, 2021

PERMISSIONS

"When Should a Man Stop Smoking Weed?" A version of this story first appeared *Playboy*, September 2013. Used with permission of the author.

"The High Life and Strange Times of the Pope of Pot." *Rolling Stone*, June 13, 1991. Used with permission of the author.

"Dab Artists." A version of this story first appeared in *California Sunday Magazine*, May 3, 2015. Used with permission of the author.

"The Trial of Hunter S. Thompson," *Rolling Stone*, June 26, 1990. Used with permission of the author.

"Charges Dropped Against Hunter Thompson," *Rolling Stone*, July 12–28, 1990. Used with permission of the author.

"The Morning Coke: On Being Hunter S. Thompson's Assistant for Three Weeks," interview by Elian Peltier for Ulyces.co, posted March 24, 2016, originally in French. Used with permission of the interviewer.

ABOUT THE AUTHOR

Mike Sager is a best-selling author and award-winning reporter. A former *Washington Post* staff writer and contributing editor to *Rolling Stone*, he has written for *Esquire* for more than thirty years. Sager is the author or editor of more than a dozen books, including anthologies, novels, a biography, and textbooks. In 2010 he won the National Magazine Award for profile writing. A number of his stories have inspired films and documentaries; he is editor and publisher of The Sager Group LLC. For more information, please see MikeSager.com.

ABOUT THE PUBLISHERS

NeoText is a publisher of quality fiction and long-form journalism. Visit the NeoText website at NeoTextCorp.com.

The Sager Group was founded in 1984. In 2012 it was chartered as a multimedia content brand, with the intent of empowering those who create art—an umbrella beneath which makers can pursue, and profit from, their craft directly, without gatekeepers. TSG publishes books; ministers to artists and provides modest grants; and produces documentary, feature, and commercial films. By harnessing the means of production, The Sager Group helps artists help themselves. For more information, please see TheSagerGroup.net.

ALSO BY MIKE SAGER

NONFICTION

Scary Monsters and Super Freaks:
Stories of Sex, Drugs, Rock 'n' Roll, and Murder

Revenge of the Donut Boys:
True Stories of Lust, Fame, Survival, and Multiple Personality

The Someone You're Not:
True Stories of Sports, Celebrity, Politics & Pornography

Stoned Again: The High Times and Strange Life of a Drugs Correspondent

Vetville: True Stories of the U.S. Marines at War and at Home

The Devil and John Holmes - 25th Anniversary Author's Edition:
And Other True Stories of Drugs, Porn and Murder

Janet's World:
The Inside Story of Washington Post Pulitzer Fabulist Janet Cooke

Travels with Bassem:
A Palestinian and a Jew Find Friendship in a War-Torn Land

The Lonely Hedonist:
True Stories of Sex, Drugs, Dinosaurs and Peter Dinklage

Tattoos & Tequila:
To Hell and Back with One of Rock's Most Notorious Frontmen

Shaman: The Mysterious Life and Impeccable Death of Carlos Castaneda

Hunting Marlon Brando: A True Story

A Boy and His Dog in Hell: And Other True Stories

The Rise and Fall of a Super Freak:
And Other True Stories of Black Men Who Made History

FICTION

Deviant Behavior, A Novel

High Tolerance, A Novel

For more information, please see MikeSager.com